™

EXPANSE

First published in the United States 2023 by Insight Editions
First published in Great Britain 2024 by Expanse
An imprint of HarperCollins*Publishers*
1 London Bridge Street, London SE1 9GF
www.farshore.co.uk

HarperCollins*Publishers*
Harper Ireland, Macken House, 39/40 Mayor Street Upper,
Dublin 1 D01 C9W8, Ireland

ISBN 978 0 00 864599 1
Printed in Malaysia
001

A CIP catalogue record for this title is available from the British Library.

MIX
Paper | Supporting
responsible forestry
FSC™ C007454

POKÉMON™
BAKING BOOK

Delightful Bakes Inspired by
the World of Pokémon

 Jarrett Melendez

Contents

Introduction

For decades, the Pokémon universe has inspired millions to be the very best they can be through embarking on adventures, building relationships with other Trainers, practising and training and, of course, collecting lots and lots of different types of Pokémon. Only by building a strong team of varied Pokémon can you achieve your goals, and that requires knowledge and patience – both of which are also needed for baking.

Just like the Pokémon you train, you'll need to learn lots of skills and techniques to master the recipes in this book. But don't worry: most recipes contained within are family-friendly and suitable for bakers of any skill level. You'll find simple cookies and brownies all the way up to challenging bakes, like a soufflé inspired by the Legendary Pokémon Koraidon, which might require a little help and a watchful eye.

The techniques of each bake aren't the only things that are wide and varied. Each recipe is inspired by different Pokémon throughout the generations and across the various regions of the Pokémon universe. There are recipes inspired by Fire-type Pokémon that contain warming spices like cinnamon and ginger to heat your bellies and hearts. Other recipes are inspired by Ice-type Pokémon, with ingredients like mint for a refreshing blast of flavour on your palate. You'll discover recipes inspired by Ground- and Rock-type Pokémon that are packed with chocolate or nuts for a dense, rich experience that'll leave you full (yet still wanting more!). Some recipes even reflect the different regions in the Pokémon universe, such as Comfey's Tropical Pavlova, which feels right at home in the tropical setting of Alola, as well as Chespin's Raspberry Pistachio Napoleons, which look elegant enough to grace the tables of the finest castles in Kalos.

The goal of this book is to capture the sense of wonder and adventure found in the Pokémon universe and transport it to the world of baking. Just like beating a tough Gym Leader in a Pokémon battle, there's nothing more satisfying than pulling off a challenging bake. So fire up the oven, get out your mixing bowls and whisks and let's get baking!

Ingredients Guide

Dark Cocoa Powder: Prized for its deep, dark colour, this type of cocoa powder turns baked goods a dramatic shade and fills them with an even deeper chocolate flavour. During processing, it is treated with an alkaline solution, which reduces the natural acidity in the chocolate, creating a smoother consistency and flavour. It can be found in speciality food or baking supply shops and online.

Butterfly Pea Flower Powder: This adorable little plant gets its name from the pea family it belongs to and its delicate blossoms shaped like – you guessed it – butterflies. Prized for the delicate blue colour they impart on drinks and food, the blossoms are often used to make tea. This all-natural food colouring bestows both a soft blue colour and a light floral flavour. The powder can be found in health food shops and speciality food shops and online.

Freeze-dried Fruit Powders: Throughout this book, you'll see blueberry powder, pineapple powder, raspberry powder and strawberry powder used in recipes. Freeze-dried fruits are becoming more popular with home bakers because they have a much more concentrated flavour, so you can use less while imparting more flavour than when baking with fruit jams or purées. While it is more common to find freeze-dried whole fruits in food shops and supermarkets, the pre-powdered forms are easy to find in health food shops and online. If you can find only the whole-fruit versions, simply grind them down in a spice grinder, with a mortar and pestle or with a trusty zip-lock food bag and rolling pin, and sift. If you have any leftover powder or larger crumbles, you can use them as snacks, blend them into smoothies or colourfully decorate your bakes with them.

Pistachio Paste: Made from peeled, roasted pistachios, this paste is packed with natural pistachio flavour. Pistachio paste is notoriously difficult to make at home because you *have* to peel each pistachio individually, by hand (there's no simple or mechanized way to do it!). Fortunately, pistachio paste can be found in speciality food shops and online.

Praline Paste: Made from toasted, caramelized hazelnuts and almonds that are ground into a fine paste, this speciality ingredient imparts delicious nutty flavour, caramel notes and richness to anything you add it to. It can be found in high-end food shops and speciality baking shops and online.

Vanilla Powder: Every single part of the vanilla bean is packed with vanilla flavour, including the waxy outer pod. Many vanilla extract producers have started drying and powdering these pods for use in baking to reduce waste and stretch each of these rare and difficult-to-grow beans a bit more. Using vanilla powder in recipes adds larger brown flecks of colour and a bit of texture while imparting the same complex vanilla flavour as extract or paste. That said, extract and paste are perfectly acceptable substitutes for any recipe that calls for vanilla powder. Vanilla powder is becoming more readily available in many food shops and speciality baking shops, as well as online.

Kanto Region

Poké Ball Conchas

Charmander Brown Butter Marmalade Financiers

Doduo Chocolate Macaroons

Pikachu Tropical Cupcakes

Ponyta Cinnamon Panna Cotta

Shellder Madeleines

Poké Ball
Conchas

One of the most important tools in any Pokémon Trainer's backpack is the Poké Ball. The sweetness of these traditional rolls rivals the sweet taste of victory you feel when catching a new Pokémon pal. Try using different colours of dye and patterns to make a variety of Poké Balls, or stick with the basic red and white design.

Difficulty: ● ● ● ○
Prep time: 40 minutes
Rest time: 2½ hours
Bake time: 1 hour
Yield: 12 conchas
Dietary notes: Vegetarian

Equipment: Food mixer, hand mixer, two baking trays, scales, 10-cm cookie cutter, instant-read thermometer, wire cooling rack

Concha Dough

2½ teaspoons active dry yeast
120 ml whole milk, lukewarm
3 large eggs, room temperature
1 tablespoon vanilla paste
100 g sugar
160 g strong white bread flour
1½ teaspoons salt
120 g unsalted butter, softened

Cookie Topping

120 g plain flour
75 g icing sugar, plus more for dusting
½ teaspoon salt
120 g unsalted butter, melted and cooled
1 teaspoon vanilla extract
Red food colouring
1 large egg

Decorations

Black fondant
White chocolate buttons

1. Whisk together the active dry yeast and milk in a small bowl. Leave to sit for about 5 minutes, until foamy. If the mixture doesn't foam, the milk may be too warm. The ideal temperature should be between 40°C and 45°C. Otherwise, the yeast may be expired, and you may need to buy new yeast.

2. Add the yeast-and-milk mixture to the bowl of a food mixer fitted with a dough hook. Add the eggs, vanilla paste, sugar, flour and salt to the bowl and mix on a low speed until moistened. Increase the speed to medium and mix for 3 to 5 minutes until a loose dough forms.

3. Add the butter, 15 g at a time, allowing the butter to fully incorporate between each addition. When you've added all the butter, increase the mixer speed to medium-high and leave to mix for 15 to 20 minutes, until the dough is still tacky but pulls away from the sides of the bowl.

4. Cover the bowl and leave to sit in a warm place for about 1 hour, until the dough has doubled in volume and looks quite puffy.

> **note:** This process, called proving, gives your bread its airy texture and flavour. During the proving process, the yeast eats the sugars in the dough and releases gas, stretching the gluten strands and making the dough puff up.

5. While the concha dough is rising, make the cookie topping. Mix the flour, icing sugar and salt in a medium bowl. Stir in the butter and vanilla until a soft dough forms.

6. Divide the cookie topping into two equal portions. Beat about 15 drops of red food colouring into one half of the mixture with a hand mixer until it is fully incorporated. Divide both the white mixture and the red mixture into 6 equal portions, for a total of 12 balls of cookie topping. Cover with cling film and set aside.

continued on the next page

7. Line 2 baking trays with baking paper. Take out the concha dough, gently punch it down to deflate and turn it out on to a generously floured surface. Weigh the dough with a digital scales and divide it into 12 equal portions. Working with one ball of dough at a time, shape the pieces into balls and then place them on your work surface. Cup your hand over the ball of dough, with your fingertips on the work surface. Move your cupped hand in a circular motion over the dough to tighten the surface and form a smooth ball. Move the shaped roll to one of the prepared trays. Repeat with the remaining dough, placing 6 rolls on each baking tray.

8. Sandwich one ball of the cookie topping between two squares of baking paper. Flatten with a heavy pan or skillet to form a round a bit larger than 10 cm across. Use a 10 cm cookie cutter to cut out a perfect circle. Cut the circle in half with a sharp knife. Repeat with all 12 balls of cookie topping.

9. In a small bowl, beat the remaining egg together with 1 tablespoon water. Brush the tops of all the concha dough balls with the egg wash. Top each piece of concha dough with one semicircle of white cookie topping, and one semicircle of red cookie topping, overlapping them by about 1 cm.

10. Let the prepared dough rise, uncovered, until doubled in size, 1 to 1½ hours. In the last half hour of rising, preheat the oven to 165°C.

11. When the dough has risen, place one baking tray of conchas in the fridge, and bake the other tray of conchas for 25 to 30 minutes until they are golden brown and the internal temperature registers at 90°C on an instant-read thermometer. Remove from the oven and let cool in the tray for 10 minutes before transferring the conchas to a wire rack to cool completely. Repeat with the remaining tray of conchas.

12. Knead the black fondant separately on a clean, dry surface until smooth and pliable. Lightly dust the surface with icing sugar and roll out the fondant (about ¼ cm thick). Cut the fondant into 12 thin strips that are as long as your conchas and about 1 cm wide.

13. Cut out 12 black circles (about 4 cm in diameter). Place a black band over the middle of each concha, where the red and white halves meet, then arrange a black circle in the centre of the concha. Place a white chocolate button in the centre of each black circle, then serve.

Charmander
Brown Butter Marmalade Financiers

Brown butter gives this bright, citrusy dessert a nutty, toasty flavour and these round, miniature cakes are loaded with a beautiful, bright orange marmalade – as bright as this beloved Fire-type Pokémon! Of course, you can make brown butter by leaving it next to a Charmander's tail, but we recommend using a saucepan on your hob instead.

Difficulty: ● ● ○ ○
Prep time: 15 minutes
Bake time: 20 minutes
Yield: 12 financiers
Dietary notes: Vegetarian

Equipment: 12-hole muffin tray, small saucepan

Financiers

120 g unsalted butter
200 g almond flour
90 g plain flour
¾ teaspoon salt
100 g sugar
6 egg whites
2 teaspoons vanilla extract
½ teaspoon almond extract

Marmalade Filling

6 tablespoons marmalade
1 teaspoon ground ginger
1 tablespoon freshly grated ginger

1. Preheat the oven to 190°C. Lightly grease a standard 12-hole muffin tray.

2. Heat the butter in a small saucepan over a medium heat. Cook, swirling the pan occasionally, until the solids turn golden brown, about 7 to 10 minutes. Leave to cool slightly.

3. Whisk together the almond flour, plain flour, salt and sugar in a large bowl. Stir in the brown butter.

4. Beat the egg whites, along with the vanilla and almond extracts, in a small bowl until quite foamy, about 1 to 2 minutes. Stir this into the flour mixture. Divide the batter among all 12 cups in the muffin tray. Set aside.

5. Prepare the marmalade filling by adding the marmalade, ground ginger and fresh ginger to a small saucepan and heating over a medium-low heat until runny, about 3 to 5 minutes. Stir to combine.

6. Use a wet finger to make a divot in the centre of each financier. Add 1½ teaspoons marmalade filling to each financier. Bake for 20 minutes until golden brown. Leave to cool in the tray for 10 minutes before transferring to a wire rack to cool further. Serve warm or at room temperature.

Doduo
Chocolate Macaroons

These chocolate macaroons are a great snack when you need a little energy boost. While they may not give you the ability to run as fast as a Doduo, they pack a chocolatey punch along with lots of coconut flavour that's sure to give you powerful strides!

Difficulty: ● ○ ○ ○
Prep time: 10 minutes
Bake time: 20 to 25 minutes
Yield: 24 macaroons
Dietary notes: Gluten-free, non-dairy, vegetarian

Equipment: Baking tray, ice-cream scoop, microwave, two piping bags

Macaroons

110 g dark chocolate, melted and cooled
30 g cocoa powder, plus more for dusting
200 g sugar
½ teaspoon salt
1½ teaspoons vanilla powder or extract
4 egg whites
300 g unsweetened shredded coconut, lightly toasted

Decorations

Flaked almonds
Black and white candy melts

1. Preheat the oven to 180°C. Line a baking tray with baking paper. Stir together the chocolate, cocoa powder, sugar, salt and vanilla in a large bowl.

2. Vigorously beat the egg whites in a separate large bowl until frothy, about 1 to 2 minutes. Stir into the chocolate mixture. Fold in the toasted coconut until well incorporated.

3. Use a ice-cream scoop to portion 24 macaroons on to the prepared baking tray. If you don't have an ice-cream scoop, measure out 2 tablespoons of mix for each cookie and roll it into a ball with your hands. Leave about 2.5 cm between each cookie – they will not spread or rise, so it's OK to fit all 24 on the same tray.

4. Bake for 20 to 25 minutes until the cookies are set but not fully dry. Leave to cool for about 10 minutes, then dust with additional cocoa powder to coat if desired. Carefully insert 2 almond flakes into each one to form Doduo's beak. If the almond slivers break too easily, poke two holes into each macaroon with a chopstick, then insert the almond slivers into the holes. Leave to cool completely and serve.

5. Place the black candy melts in a microwave-safe bowl. Heat for 30 seconds at a time until the candy is fully melted. Stir until smooth, then pour into a piping bag.

6. Cut off the tip of the piping bag to create a small opening. Pipe 48 small circles on to the baking paper and leave to set for a few minutes. These will be Doduo's eyes.

7. Repeat step 5 with the white candy melts in a clean piping bag. Cut off the tip of the piping bag to create a very small opening and pipe a small white dot on the set black eyes to complete Doduo's eyes.

8. Assemble each macaroon using the eyes you made with the candy melts. Leave the macaroons to cool completely, then serve.

Pikachu
Tropical Cupcakes

These brightly coloured cupcakes are full of delicious tropical flavour. The coconut cupcake base is as sweet as a Pikachu's face, while the pineapple frosting is reminiscent of the iconic Mouse Pokémon and packed with enough tartness to give your tongue a little zap. Eating just one of these cupcakes will put you in the mood to surf the waves!

Difficulty: ● ● ○ ○
Prep time: 45 minutes
Bake time: 30 minutes
Yield: 12 cupcakes
Dietary notes: Vegetarian

Equipment: 12-hole muffin tray, food mixer, wire cooling rack, hand mixer, five piping bags (one with 1-cm round tip), baking tray

Cupcakes
240 g plain flour
¾ teaspoon baking powder
½ teaspoon bicarbonate of soda
½ teaspoon salt
240 g unsalted butter, room temperature
300 g sugar
3 large eggs, room temperature
2 teaspoons vanilla extract
180 ml buttermilk, room temperature
225 g unsweetened shredded coconut, toasted

Frosting
200 g icing sugar
120 g unsalted butter, softened
3 tablespoons pineapple powder
2 teaspoons lemon juice
30 ml double cream
Yellow food colouring

Decorations
Black, white, yellow and red candy melts

To make the cupcakes:

1. Preheat the oven to 165°C. Line a standard muffin tray with 12 paper cupcake cases.

2. Whisk together the flour, baking powder, bicarbonate of soda and salt in a medium bowl until combined. Set aside.

3. Cream together the butter and sugar in the bowl of a food mixer fitted with a paddle attachment. Beat at a medium speed until light and fluffy, about 5 to 7 minutes. Add the eggs, one at a time, beating until fully incorporated before adding the next egg. Add the vanilla and beat to combine.

4. Reduce the mixer speed to low. Add a third of the flour mixture, beat to combine, then add a third of the buttermilk. Repeat with the remaining flour mixture and buttermilk. Turn off the mixer and fold in the toasted coconut with a plastic spatula.

5. Pour the batter into the prepared muffin tray. Bake for 25 to 30 minutes until the cupcakes are golden brown on top and a cake tester or toothpick inserted into the cakes comes out clean. Let the cupcakes cool in the tray for 10 minutes before transferring them to a wire rack to cool completely.

To make the frosting:

6. Add the icing sugar, butter and pineapple powder to a large bowl. Mix with a hand mixer on a low speed until the icing sugar is moistened, then increase the speed to medium-high and beat for about 8 minutes, until light and fluffy. Add the lemon juice and mix for about 1 minute to combine, then add the double cream 1 tablespoon at a time and mix until perfectly smooth. Mix in yellow food colouring as needed to achieve the perfect Pikachu colour.

note: If you can't find freeze-dried pineapple or pineapple powder, omit the double cream and use 2 tablespoons of pineapple juice. If using pineapple juice, make sure to bring to a simmer for a few minutes in a small saucepan to denature the enzymes, or your frosting will curdle. You could also use previously frozen juice.

continued on the next page

To assemble:

7. Add the frosting to a piping bag fitted with a 1-cm round tip. Hold the piping bag over each cupcake and pipe a medium-size swirl of frosting on to the cupcake. Flip the cupcake upside down on to a piece of wax paper and carefully smush the cupcake down, spreading the frosting flat across the top of the cupcake. If necessary, use a knife or an offset spatula to smooth the edges of the frosting around the cupcake. Chill the cupcakes in the fridge for 5 to 10 minutes.

8. Line a baking tray with baking paper.

9. Place the black candy melts in a microwave-safe bowl. Heat for 30 seconds at a time until the candy is fully melted. Stir until smooth, then pour into a piping bag, reserving some for dipping (see step 12).

10. Cut off the tip of the piping bag to create a small opening. Pipe 24 circles on to the baking paper and leave to set for a few minutes. These will be Pikachu's eyes. Use the remaining black melts to pipe the 12 noses and 12 mouths.

11. Repeat the melting instructions in step 9 with the white candy melts in a clean piping bag. Cut off the tip of the piping bag to create a very small opening and pipe a small white dot on the set black eyes to complete Pikachu's eyes.

12. Repeat the melting instructions in step 9 with the yellow candy melts. Pipe 24 long, thin ovular shapes that are about 5-6 cm inches long and that follow the shape of Pikachu's ears, becoming widest in the middle and tapering to a point at the end. These will be Pikachu's ears. Leave to set. When they are set, dip the ends in the reserved black candy melts at an angle, so that the black part takes up about a third of the ear and is longer on the outside of the ear compared to the inside.

13. Repeat the melting instructions in step 9 with the red candy melts. Pipe 24 small circles, larger than the eyes, these will be the red dots on Pikachu's cheeks.

14. Assemble each cupcake using the eyes, noses, mouths and cheek dots you made with the candy melts. Place the eyes in the centre vertically, with the ears sticking out of the top of the cupcake above the eyes at an angle. Place the two cheeks on the lower curves of the face below the eyes. Place the nose between the eyes horizontally, and between the eyes and cheeks vertically. Finally, place the mouth between the cheeks, set just above their centre.

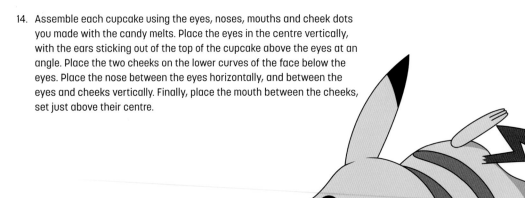

Ponyta
Cinnamon Panna Cotta

The not-so-secret ingredient in this sweetened cream dessert is cinnamon, which gives the custard a pleasant warmth. It's cool to the touch, which may seem strange for a Fire-type Pokémon – but Ponyta's fiery mane won't burn you either, after it learns to trust you! Top your panna cotta with candied orange zest shaped in a flame motif for a flashy finish.

Difficulty: ● ● ○ ○
Prep time: 20 minutes
Cook time: 15 minutes
Chill time: 5 to 29 hours
Yield: Serves 6
Dietary notes: Gluten-free

Equipment: Medium saucepan, six small dessert bowls

Base
180 ml double cream
240 ml whole milk
50 g sugar
¼ teaspoon salt
4 cinnamon sticks

Gelatin Mixture
2 teaspoons gelatin granules
120 ml whole milk

Decoration
Candied orange peel

1. Whisk the double cream, whole milk, sugar and salt in a medium saucepan. Add the cinnamon sticks and cook over a medium heat for about 5 to 7 minutes, stirring occasionally, until the liquid just begins to steam. Remove from the heat and leave to steep for at least 1 hour at room temperature, or for up to 24 hours covered and chilled in the fridge.

2. Prepare the gelatin by sprinkling the gelatin granules over the 120 ml whole milk. Let the gelatin granules hydrate for 5 minutes. Stir to combine, then add the milk-and-gelatin mixture to the saucepan with the chilled double cream mixture. Heat over a medium heat until just beginning to simmer, about 6 to 8 minutes, but do not let it boil. Remove from heat.

3. Divide the mixture among six small dessert bowls. Cover with cling film and chill for at least 4 hours to set.

4. Cut the candied orange peel into spear shapes of different lengths. Gently place on top of the set panna cotta, arranging the spears to look like the end of Ponyta's flaming tail. Serve chilled.

Shellder
Madeleines

These tender, little shell-shaped cakes are made with a special madeleine tray to create the distinctive Shellder shape. This classic French dessert is sweetened with honey and spiked with orange zest for a delicately floral, citrusy flavour, which is rounded out with a purple-tinted white chocolate dipping sauce to emulate the beloved Bivalve Pokémon.

Difficulty: ● ● ● ○
Prep time: 15 minutes
Bake time: 10 to 12 minutes
Yield: 12 madeleines
Dietary notes: Vegetarian

Equipment: 12-cake madeleine tray, piping bag, microwave

Madeleines

120 g plain flour, plus more for dusting
1 teaspoon baking powder
¾ teaspoon salt
2 large eggs, room temperature
2 tablespoons honey
Zest of 1 orange
105 g unsalted butter, melted, plus more for the tray

White Chocolate Dipping Sauce

170 g white chocolate
1 tablespoon butterfly pea flower powder, or a couple of drops of blue food colouring
1 drop red food colouring

1. Preheat the oven to 200°C. Generously butter a 12-cake madeleine tray. Dust with flour, then tap out the excess.

2. Whisk together the flour, baking powder and salt in a small bowl. In a medium bowl, beat the eggs, honey and orange zest until smooth. Stir in the flour mixture. Continue stirring as you slowly drizzle the butter into the bowl until it's fully incorporated.

3. Pour the batter into a piping bag. If the batter is quite runny, chill in the fridge for at least an hour. Otherwise, cut off the tip of the bag to make a 1-cm opening, then pipe the batter into the prepared madeleine tray and bake for 10 to 12 minutes, until the cakes are golden brown.

4. As the madeleines bake, prepare the dipping sauce. Add the white chocolate to a small microwave-safe bowl. Microwave for 30 seconds, stir and repeat until the chocolate is fully melted and smooth. Stir in the butterfly pea flower powder and red food colouring a little at a time until the chocolate is fully mixed and the purple Shellder colour is achieved. Serve alongside the warm madeleines.

Johto Region

Phanpy Orange Cream Tartlets

Togepi Confetti Mug Cake

Chikorita Cheesy
Pesto Brioche Rolls

Igglybuff Chocolate
Raspberry Cupcakes

Delibird Red Velvet Cake
with Peppermint
Cream Cheese Frosting

Blissey Strawberry Twists

Magby Spicy Cherry
Tomato Galette

Phanpy
Orange Cream Tartlets

*These tiny tarts have an orange-flavoured crust
and a colourful vanilla custard filling. They're
finished with a strip of candied orange peel to tie
the flavours together and match the cute orange
stripe on Phanpy's trunk. Like Phanpy, these tarts
may be small, but they pack a (citrusy) punch – and,
thankfully, these tarts won't send you flying!*

Difficulty: ● ● ○ ○
Prep time: 15 minutes
Chill time: 3 hours
Cook time: 35 minutes
Yield: 12 mini tarts
Dietary notes: Vegetarian

Equipment: Medium saucier, fine
mesh sieve, food mixer, 12-hole
muffin tray, 10-cm cookie cutter,
wire cooling rack, offset spatula

Custard
3 large egg whites
150 g sugar
1 teaspoon vanilla extract
180 ml double cream
180 ml whole milk
30 g unsalted butter
2 to 3 drops blue food colouring (optional)

Crust
180 g plain flour
25 g icing sugar
½ teaspoon salt
2 teaspoons orange zest
120 g unsalted butter,
cut into 1-cm cubes
1 tablespoon orange juice
30 ml double cream
Red and yellow food colouring (optional)

Decoration
Dried papaya, cut into thin 5-cm-long strips

To make the custard:

1. To make the custard, add the egg whites, sugar and vanilla to a medium
    bowl. Vigorously whisk the mixture until it's pale and thick.

2. Bring the double cream and milk to a bare simmer over a medium heat
    in a medium saucier, stirring occasionally. Begin whisking the egg white
    mixture. While whisking continuously, pour in the hot milk mixture in a
    slow, gentle drizzle, a little bit at a time, until fully incorporated.

note: Sauciers have a curved bottom, which makes them preferable
when a mixture will likely get trapped in the edges of a straight-sided
saucepan. A saucepan is okay to use if you don't have a saucier, but
you'll have to be extra vigilant and thorough with stirring so that the
mixture doesn't get trapped in the edges and burn.

3. Return the mixture to the saucier and warm it over a medium-low heat,
    whisking constantly, until the mixture thickens and begins to bubble. Once
    you see the first bubble, set a 1-minute timer and continue whisking. When
    the minute is up, remove from the heat and pour through a fine mesh sieve
    set over a medium bowl. Whisk in the butter and blue food colouring (if
    using) until smooth. Cover with cling film, pushing the plastic directly on to
    the custard (to prevent a skin from forming) and chill for at least 3 hours.

To make the crust:

4. Add the flour, icing sugar, salt, orange zest and butter to the bowl of a food
    mixer. Pulse until the mixture resembles wet sand. Tip the contents of the
    bowl into a large mixing bowl.

5. Stir together the orange juice, double cream, 1 drop of red food colouring,
    and 5 drops of yellow food colouring (if using) in a small bowl. Add to the
    flour mixture and stir with a wooden spoon until a firm dough forms. Wrap
    in cling film and chill for at least 1 hour.

continued on the next page

To finish and assemble:

6. Preheat the oven to 180°C. Lightly grease a standard 12-hole muffin tray.

7. Begin assembling the tarts in the last 30 minutes of the custard's chill time. Place the prepared tart dough on a lightly floured surface. Roll out to a thickness of about ½ cm, then use a 10-cm cookie cutter to cut out 12 rounds. If necessary, knead the scraps together, reroll to a thickness of ½ cm, and repeat until you have 12 rounds.

8. Gently press the dough into the cups of the muffin tin, making sure the dough is uniform and flat against the insides of the cups.

9. Line each tart shell with a square of foil and fill with uncooked rice or beans – this will prevent the tart shells from puffing up in the oven. Bake for 15 minutes. Remove the beans (or rice) and foil, then bake for 5 to 8 more minutes until golden brown. Leave to cool in the tray for 15 minutes, then loosen with a thin knife to remove. Transfer to a wire cooling rack to cool completely.

10. Fill each tart shell with the cooled custard. Smooth over the tops with an offset spatula, then place a strip of dried papaya across the centre of each tart. Transfer the finished tarts to a serving plate, cover with foil or cling film, and keep chilled until ready to serve.

Togepi
Confetti Mug Cake

This petite cake is simple and quick to make, perfect for those times when your sweet tooth strikes and you need dessert in a hurry. This sweet, vanilla-flavoured cake is full of brightly coloured sprinkles to emulate Togepi's cute appearance. It's also warm and comforting right out of the microwave, like the happiness that Togepi stores in its shell.

Difficulty: ● ○ ○ ○
Prep time: 5 minutes
Cook time: 2 minutes
Yield: 1 mug cake
Dietary notes: Vegetarian

Equipment: 340-ml mug, microwave

Mug Cake

15 g unsalted butter
30 g sugar
½ teaspoon vanilla extract
¼ teaspoon salt
15 ml whole milk
1 large egg
30 g plain flour
¼ teaspoon baking powder
1½ tablespoons sprinkles

To Serve

Vanilla ice cream
Sprinkles

1. Add the butter to a 340-ml mug. Heat in the microwave on high in 5-second intervals until the butter is soft and beginning to melt. Stir in the sugar, vanilla, salt and milk. Beat in the egg until smooth, about 1 minute. Stir in the flour, baking powder and sprinkles.

2. Microwave for 1 minute to 1 minute and 20 seconds until the cake is puffed and set. Serve warm with a scoop of vanilla ice cream on top and additional sprinkles, as desired.

Chikorita
Cheesy Pesto Brioche Rolls

These brioche rolls are packed with cheese and flavourful pesto, making them great for an afternoon snack or as an accompaniment to your favourite pasta dish. Each one is topped with a fresh basil leaf while the rolls are still warm, which gives off a pleasant smell, just like the leaf on Chikorita's head.

Difficulty: ● ● ○ ○
Prep time: 30 minutes
Rest time: 3½ hours
Bake time: 30 minutes
Yield: 12 rolls
Dietary notes: Vegetarian*

*if vegetarian alternative used for Parmesan cheese

Equipment: Food mixer, 12-hole muffin tray, wire cooling rack

Brioche

240 ml whole milk, lukewarm
480 g plain flour, plus more for dusting
1 tablespoon instant yeast
2½ teaspoons salt
30 g sugar
3 large eggs
120 g unsalted butter, softened

Filling

One 170g jar pesto
225 g shredded mozzarella cheese
25 g grated Parmesan cheese,
or vegetarian alternative
12 fresh basil leaves

note: If you're unsure whether the dough is ready in step 2, tear off a small chunk. Stretch the dough – if you can stretch it enough to see through it without the dough tearing, it's ready to go. If the dough tears, continue mixing for 5 more minutes, then test it again. (This is called the windowpane test.)

1. Add the milk, flour, yeast, salt and sugar to the bowl of a food mixer fitted with a dough hook attachment. Mix on a low speed until a shaggy dough forms (the dough will be lumpy, with no dry flour remaining). Add the eggs, one at a time, mixing continuously; wait for each egg to completely incorporate before adding the next one. Increase the mixer speed to medium and mix until the dough is smooth, about 5 minutes.

2. Add the butter 30 g at a time, allowing the butter to incorporate between each addition. Mix for about 15 more minutes, until the dough is smooth, glossy and elastic.

3. Place the dough in a lightly oiled bowl and cover. Leave to rise for 1½ to 2 hours until the dough is quite puffy and has nearly doubled in volume. Lightly grease a standard muffin tray.

4. Tip out the dough on to a lightly floured surface and gently press it down to deflate. Sprinkle a small amount of flour over the top of the dough, then roll it out into a 33-by-40-cm rectangle.

5. Spread the pesto over the surface of the dough, leaving a 2½-cm border along one of the shorter sides. Sprinkle the mozzarella and Parmesan cheese over the pesto, leaving the same 2½-cm border clean. Starting at the short side *without* the clean border, roll the dough into a tight log, ending at the clean border. Pinch the dough to seal.

6. Trim 1 cm off each end of the log, then cut it into twelve 2½-cm-thick discs. Place 1 disc in each prepared muffin cup. Lightly cover the muffin tray with cling film and let the dough rise for 1 to 1½ hours, until it's quite puffy. Towards the end of the rising time, preheat the oven to 180°C.

7. Bake for 25 to 30 minutes or until the internal temperature registers 90°C on an instant-read thermometer inserted into the centre of each roll.

8. Leave the rolls to cool for 5 minutes in the tray before transferring them to a wire rack to cool until they're just warm enough to eat comfortably. Insert a fresh basil leaf into the centre of each roll and take a calming breath of fresh, warm basil scent. Serve warm or at room temperature.

Igglybuff
Chocolate Raspberry Cupcakes

Igglybuff are known for releasing a sweet, calming aroma to soothe their foes and others around them. These cupcakes may not smell quite like Igglybuff, but this blend of chocolate and raspberry is just the sweet thing to soothe your nerves after a long day.

Difficulty: ● ● ○ ○
Prep time: 15 minutes
Bake time: 25 minutes
Yield: 12 cupcakes
Dietary notes: Vegetarian

Equipment: 12-hole muffin tray, food mixer, wire cooling rack, hand mixer, two piping bags (one with 1-cm round tip), microwave

Cupcakes

120 g plain flour
60 g cocoa powder
1 teaspoon baking powder
½ teaspoon bicarbonate of soda
½ teaspoon salt
1 teaspoon espresso powder
2 large eggs, room temperature
1 large egg yolk, room temperature
100 g sugar
60 g unsalted butter,
room temperature
60 ml neutral oil, such as vegetable
1 tablespoon vanilla extract
180 ml sour cream

Frosting

200 g icing sugar
120 g unsalted butter, softened
1½ tablespoons raspberry powder or
3 tablespoons raspberry jam
1 teaspoon lemon juice
30 ml double cream
60 g dark chocolate

note: To ensure neat spirals, you can also pipe the chocolate on to a sheet of baking paper. Chill the chocolate in the refrigerator until the chocolate hardens (10 to 20 minutes), then carefully transfer to the top of the cupcake.

1. Preheat the oven to 180°C. Line a standard muffin tray with 12 paper cupcake cases. Whisk together the flour, cocoa powder, baking powder, bicarbonate of soda, salt and espresso powder in a large bowl.

2. Add the eggs, egg yolk, sugar, butter, oil and vanilla to the bowl of a food mixer fitted with a paddle attachment. Beat on a medium speed for about 5 minutes, until smooth.

3. Reduce the mixer speed to low, then add half of the flour mixture and mix until just combined. Add the sour cream, mixing to combine. Add the remaining flour mixture and mix until no dry flour is visible. Scrape down the sides and bottom of the bowl with a plastic spatula to ensure that the batter is fully mixed.

4. Divide the batter evenly among the 12 cupcake cases and bake for 20 to 25 minutes or until a cake tester comes out clean when inserted into the centres of the cupcakes. Let the cupcakes cool in the tray for 10 minutes before transferring them to a wire rack to cool completely.

5. Make the frosting while the cupcakes cool. Add the icing sugar, butter and raspberry powder to a large bowl. Mix with a hand mixer on a low speed until the icing sugar is moistened, then increase the speed to medium-high and beat for about 8 minutes, until light and fluffy. Add the lemon juice and mix for about 1 minute to combine, then add the double cream 1 tablespoon at a time, mixing until perfectly smooth.

6. Add the frosting to a piping bag fitted with a 1-cm round tip. Pipe a round mound of frosting on to each cupcake. Flip the cupcake upside down on to a piece of wax paper and carefully smush the cupcake down, spreading the frosting flat across the top of the cupcake. If necessary, use a knife or an offset spatula to smooth the edges of the frosting around the cupcake. Chill the cupcakes in the fridge for 5 to 10 minutes.

7. Place the dark chocolate in a microwave-safe bowl. Heat for 30 seconds at a time, stirring each time, until the chocolate is melted and smooth. Pour the chocolate into a piping bag and let it cool slightly – it should still be liquid, but not hot, or the chocolate will melt the frosting.

8. Pipe a chocolate spiral on each cupcake for the spiral on Igglybuff's head.

Delibird
Red Velvet Cake
with Peppermint Cream Cheese Frosting

Although most red velvet cakes are topped with plain cream cheese frosting, this one has peppermint for a nice cooling effect to match Delibird's Ice-type nature. The size of this cake is perfect for sharing because the Delivery Pokémon generously shares its food with people and Pokémon alike.

Difficulty: ● ● ○ ○
Prep time: 30 minutes
Bake time: 30 minutes
Yield: Serves 12 to 16
Dietary notes: Vegetarian

Equipment: Two 20-cm round cake tins, food mixer, wire cooling racks, hand mixer, offset spatula, food processor, piping bags with large round tip and small star tip

Cake
240 g self-raising flour
3 tablespoons cocoa powder
1 teaspoon bicarbonate of soda
2 eggs
300 g sugar
120 g unsalted butter, melted and cooled
1 teaspoon salt
1 tablespoon vinegar
1 tablespoon vanilla extract
1½ tablespoons red food colouring
240 ml buttermilk

Frosting
200 g icing sugar
450 g cream cheese, softened
120 g unsalted butter, softened
1 teaspoon vanilla extract
2 teaspoons peppermint extract

Decorations
Peppermint sweets
Black and yellow sugar sprinkles (optional)

To make the cake:

1. Preheat the oven to 180°C. Grease two 20-cm cake tins, and line the bottoms with a circle of baking paper. Grease the baking paper.

2. Whisk together the flour, cocoa powder and bicarbonate of soda in a small bowl. Set aside.

3. Add the eggs and sugar to the bowl of a food mixer fitted with a paddle attachment. Beat on a medium speed until the mixture is pale and thick. Add the butter, salt, vinegar, vanilla and red food colouring, mixing until fully combined.

4. Reduce the mixer speed to low and add a third of the flour mixture. Mix until just combined, then add half the buttermilk. Repeat with the remaining flour mixture and buttermilk, making sure that the flour mixture is the last addition. Mix until no dry flour remains. Scrape the sides and bottom of the bowl with a plastic spatula to ensure that the batter is fully mixed.

5. Divide the batter between the two cake tins. Smooth the top of the batter, then bake for 30 minutes or until a cake tester inserted into the centre of the cakes comes out clean. Let the cakes cool for 15 minutes in the tins, then transfer them to a wire rack to cool completely.

To make the frosting:

6. Make the frosting as the cakes cool. Add the icing sugar, cream cheese, butter, vanilla and peppermint extract to a large bowl. Beat with a hand mixer until completely smooth, about 10 minutes.

To decorate:

7. If the cakes have domed, use a long serrated knife to trim the domed top off each cake so they are flat and level. Place one of the cooled cakes on a plate and add a bit of frosting to the top. Spread into an even layer with an offset spatula, then place the second cake on top. Add more frosting to the top and spread it evenly over the top and sides, adding more frosting as needed, but reserving some to decorate the top.

8. Crush peppermint sweets in a food processor until they are relatively fine, but not powdered. (It's OK to have some larger crunchy bits.) Press the crushed candies into the frosting on the side of the cake.

9. Add about three quarters of the remaining frosting to a piping bag fitted with a large round tip. Pipe one 10-cm-tall mound in the middle of the top of the cake. This is the bottom of Delibird's sack.

10. Line a small baking tray or plate with baking paper. Add the remaining frosting to a small piping bag fitted with a small star tip. Pipe a smaller mound on to the baking paper and freeze it for 15 minutes or until firm enough to handle without losing its shape.

11. Peel the frozen mound off the baking paper, and then invert it on to the round mound on the cake. The flat side of the frozen mound should be facing up, creating the top half of Delibird's sack.

12. If desired, sprinkle black and yellow sugar sprinkles over the top of the cake around the sack. Cut and serve.

Blissey
Strawberry Twists

Blissey are kind-hearted and love helping and healing others, whether human or other Pokémon. These sweet strawberry twists don't have any healing powers, but they're a lovely cure for a sweet tooth – and they're pink, just like Blissey! This recipe makes enough to share, in case you want to deliver joy to others as the Happiness Pokémon does.

Difficulty: ● ● ○ ○
Prep time: 35 minutes
Rest time: 2 hours
Bake time: 25 minutes
Yield: 12 rolls
Dietary notes: Vegetarian

Equipment: Food mixer, pizza cutter, 12-hole muffin tray, wire cooling rack, wire mesh sieve

Twists

480 g plain flour
½ teaspoon salt
240 ml milk
60 g unsalted butter, softened
2 teaspoons instant yeast
2 tablespoons maple syrup
2 eggs
110 g strawberry jam

To Finish

1 egg
Demerara sugar
50 g icing sugar
1 tablespoon strawberry powder
Whipped cream

1. Add the flour, salt, milk, butter, yeast and maple syrup to the bowl of a food mixer fitted with a dough hook attachment. Mix on a low speed until moistened, then increase the speed to medium and mix until a shaggy dough forms (the dough will be lumpy, with no dry flour remaining).

2. Add 1 egg to the bowl and allow the mixer to run until the egg is fully incorporated. Repeat with the remaining egg. Increase the speed to medium-high and knead for 15 more minutes.

3. Cover the bowl and set it in a warm spot in the kitchen for 1 hour or until the dough has doubled in volume.

> **note:** If you're unsure whether the dough is ready, tear off a small chunk. Stretch the dough – if you can stretch it enough to see through it without the dough tearing, it's ready to go. If the dough tears, continue mixing for 5 more minutes, then test it again. (This is called the windowpane test.)

4. Turn out the dough on to a floured surface. Press down on the dough gently to deflate, then roll it into a 30-by-60-cm rectangle. Spread the strawberry jam over the surface, leaving a 1-cm border around the dough. Lightly wet the border with damp fingers, then fold the dough in half into a 30-by-30-cm square, firmly pressing the edges to seal.

5. Use a pizza cutter to cut the folded dough into twelve 2½-cm-wide strips. Let the dough rest while you grease a standard muffin tray.

6. Hold the dough with one short end in each hand. Twist the dough strands together, then coil the dough into one of the prepared muffin tray cups, tucking the ends underneath the coil. Repeat with the remaining strips of dough.

continued on the next page

7. Loosely cover the muffin tray with greased cling film and let the dough rise for 1 hour, or until it's quite puffy and has roughly doubled in volume. Towards the end of this hour, preheat the oven to 180°C.

8. Beat the egg with 1 tablespoon water. Brush the tops of each roll with the egg mixture, then sprinkle liberally with demerara sugar. Bake for 20 to 25 minutes or until an instant-read thermometer registers 90°C when inserted into the centre of the rolls.

9. Let the twists cool for 10 minutes in the tray, then transfer them to a wire rack to cool completely. To finish, sift 50 g icing sugar with 1 tablespoon strawberry powder over a bowl. Transfer to a wire mesh sieve and sift over the tops of the cooled rolls to coat them in a sweet strawberry-flavoured powder. Top each roll with a dollop of whipped cream, sprinkle more icing sugar if desired, and serve.

Magby
Spicy Cherry Tomato Galette

Galettes are like a free form pie with no pie plate, but they follow the same basic recipe as a pie: crust and filling. The filling is savoury, with a nice touch of heat and smoky flavour to match Magby's fiery nature, and the cherry tomatoes piled in the centre look like Magby's head poking out of the centre of the galette.

Difficulty: ● ● ○ ○
Prep time: 20 minutes
Rest time: 1 hour
Bake time: 35 minutes
Yield: 1 galette, serves 8
Dietary notes: Vegetarian*

*if vegetarian alternative used for Parmesan cheese

Equipment: Food processor, baking tray, wire cooling rack

Crust
150 g plain flour
45 g semolina
25 g grated Parmesan cheese, or vegetarian alternative
120 g butter, cut into 1-cm cubes
½ teaspoon salt

Filling
220 g ricotta cheese
1 teaspoon lemon zest
1 teaspoon salt
¼ teaspoon black pepper
½ teaspoon garlic powder
¼ teaspoon onion powder
¼ teaspoon oregano
2 large eggs, divided
450 g cherry tomatoes, halved
½ teaspoon smoked paprika
¼ teaspoon cayenne
1 tablespoon Calabrian chillis
1 tablespoon olive oil
Smoked flaky sea salt

note: If you can't find Calabrian chillis, use 1 tablespoon spicy chipotle paste.

1. Add the flour, semolina, Parmesan cheese, butter and salt to the bowl of a food processor. Pulse until the mixture resembles wet sand. Tip the mixture into a bowl and add 1 to 2 tablespoons of cold water. Mix to form a soft dough, shape into a disc, wrap in cling film, and chill in the fridge for 1 hour.

2. Meanwhile, prepare the filling. Add the ricotta cheese, lemon zest, ½ teaspoon salt, pepper, garlic powder, onion powder, oregano and one of the eggs to a medium bowl. Whisk with a fork until smooth.

3. In a separate large bowl, add the cherry tomatoes, remaining ½ teaspoon salt, smoked paprika, cayenne, Calabrian chillis, and olive oil. Toss to coat. Set aside.

4. Preheat the oven to 220°C. Line a baking tray with baking paper.

5. Place the prepared dough on a floured surface. Roll out the dough to a circle with a thickness of about ½ cm. Transfer the dough to the prepared baking tray. Spread the ricotta filling in the centre of the dough, leaving about a 5-cm border of clean dough around the filling.

6. Spoon the tomato filling over the ricotta mixture, piling a few tomatoes higher in the centre to form the top of Magby's head. Fold the dough up over the filling, pleating every 8 or 10 cm. Beat the remaining egg together with 1 tablespoon water and brush it on the top of the crust, then sprinkle smoked sea salt over the crust and filling.

7. Bake the galette for 30 to 35 minutes, until the tomatoes burst and the filling is bubbling. Cool in the tray for 15 minutes. Serve while still warm, or transfer to a wire rack to cool completely before serving.

Hoenn Region

Seedot Black Sesame
Swirl Cake

Zigzagoon Mocha Éclairs

Taillow Chocolate Cherry
Olive Oil Cake

Whismur Lemon-Lavender Bars

Spoink Black Sesame
Cream Puffs

Flygon Pan Pizza

Seedot

Black Sesame Swirl Cake

Seedot love to prank other Pokémon by pretending to be nuts hanging in trees. The black sesame paste, almond extract and crunchy sesame topping of this cake make it taste about as yummy as the nuts Seedot pretend to be.

Difficulty: ●●○○
Prep time: 15 minutes
Bake time: 35 minutes
Yield: Serves 12 to 16
Dietary notes: Vegetarian

Equipment: 22-cm cake ring tin, food mixer, microwave, wire cooling rack, piping bag

Cake

240 g plain flour
1 teaspoon baking powder
½ teaspoon bicarbonate of soda
½ teaspoon salt
½ teaspoon cinnamon
¼ teaspoon ground cardamom
¼ teaspoon ground nutmeg
150 g unsalted butter, softened
200 g sugar
4 tablespoons black sesame paste
2 large eggs
2 teaspoons vanilla extract
½ teaspoon almond extract
240 g plain yogurt (not Greek)

Streusel Topping

165 g light brown sugar
90 g plain flour
1 teaspoon cinnamon
½ teaspoon cardamom
¼ teaspoon salt
1 tablespoon black sesame seeds
1 tablespoon white sesame seeds
1 tablespoon black sesame paste
60 g unsalted butter, melted

Decoration

60 g dark chocolate

To make the cake:

1. Preheat the oven to 180°C. Grease a 22-cm cake ring tin. Whisk together the flour, baking powder, bicarbonate of soda, salt, cinnamon, cardamom and nutmeg in a medium bowl. Set aside.
2. Add the butter, sugar and black sesame paste in the bowl of a food mixer fitted with a paddle attachment. Cream together on a medium speed until light and fluffy, about 5 to 7 minutes.
3. Add the eggs, one at a time, beating to incorporate before adding the next one. Mix in the vanilla and almond extracts.
4. Reduce the mixer speed to low. Add one third of the flour mixture and beat to incorporate. Add half of the yogurt, beating to incorporate. Repeat with the remaining two thirds of the flour mixture and half of the yogurt, beating until incorporated and no dry pockets of flour remain. Pour the batter into the prepared cake ring tin. Set aside.

To make the streusel topping:

5. Stir together the brown sugar, flour, cinnamon, cardamom, salt and black and white sesame seeds in a medium bowl. In a separate small bowl, stir together the black sesame paste and the butter until smooth. If the sesame paste is stiff, microwave it for about 30 seconds before attempting to stir it with the butter.
6. Stir the butter-and-sesame-paste mixture into the brown sugar mixture until crumbly. Scatter over the top of the cake batter. Bake for 30 to 35 minutes. Let the cake cool in the tin for 10 to 15 minutes, then transfer it to a wire rack to cool completely.

To decorate:

7. Place the dark chocolate in a microwave-safe bowl. Heat for 30 seconds at a time, stirring each time, until the chocolate is melted and smooth. Pour the chocolate into a piping bag and snip off the end to create a small hole.
8. Pipe two concentric circles on the top of the cake to match the design on Seedot's head.

Zigzagoon
Mocha Éclairs

Zigzagoon are wonderfully curious Pokémon and move in a zigzag pattern between the things that catch their interest. These éclairs not only feature a zigzag pattern on top, but they also pack a chocolate punch. They taste so good, you'll be running as fast as a Zigzagoon to grab a second helping!

Difficulty: ● ● ● ○
Prep time: 45 minutes
Bake time: 40 minutes
Rest time: 80 minutes
Chill time: 4 hours
Yield: 10 to 12 éclairs
Dietary notes: Vegetarian

Equipment: Medium saucepan, fine mesh sieve, medium saucier, instant-read thermometer, food mixer, baking tray, four piping bags (with large star tip, two flat tips and filling tip) wire cooling rack

Mocha Crème Pâtissière

360 ml whole milk
60 ml double cream
1½ teaspoons espresso powder
100 g sugar
3 tablespoons cornflour
4 large egg yolks
1 teaspoon vanilla extract
110 g dark chocolate, chopped

Choux Pastry

240 ml whole milk
90 g unsalted butter
1 tablespoon sugar
¾ teaspoon salt
120 g plain flour, sifted
4 large eggs

Icing

1¼ teaspoons espresso powder
1¼ teaspoons hot water
125 g icing sugar
1¼ tablespoons light corn syrup
1¼ teaspoons vanilla extract
3 to 4 tablespoons double cream

note: For chocolate lovers, remove the espresso powder from the crème pâtissière and replace the espresso powder in the icing with cocoa powder.

To make the mocha crème pâtissière:

1. Bring the milk, double cream and espresso powder to a bare simmer in a medium saucepan over a medium heat, stirring occasionally. Remove from heat.

2. In a medium bowl, whisk together the sugar and cornflour. Add the egg yolks and whisk until smooth. While whisking constantly, slowly pour the milk and cream mixture into the cornflour mixture.

3. Pour this mixture back into the saucepan and return it to a medium heat. Whisk constantly until the mixture begins to bubble. The moment you see it bubble, set a 1-minute timer and continue to whisk constantly. Remove from heat.

4. Add the vanilla and chocolate to a medium bowl, then set a fine mesh sieve over the bowl. Pour the crème pâtissière through the fine mesh sieve, pushing it through with a plastic spatula. Leave the crème pâtissière to sit for 3 to 5 minutes to allow the chocolate to melt, then stir. Leave to cool for 20 minutes at room temperature before covering it and chilling for at least 4 hours.

To make the choux pastry:

5. While the crème pâtissière chills, make the éclair shells. Bring the milk, butter, sugar and salt to a boil in a medium saucier over a high heat. Remove from heat and vigorously stir in the flour with a wooden spoon until smooth.

note: Sauciers have a curved bottom, which makes them preferable when a mixture will likely get trapped in the edges of a straight-sided saucepan. A saucepan is okay to use if you don't have a saucier, but you'll have to be extra vigilant and thorough with stirring so that the mixture doesn't get trapped in the edges and burn.

6. Return the saucier to a high heat and continue stirring vigorously until an instant-read thermometer registers 75°C when inserted into the mixture.

continued on the next page

7. Tip the mixture into the bowl of a food mixer fitted with a paddle attachment. Beat on a medium speed until the temperature drops to 60°C or lower. Start taking the temperature after about 3 minutes, then continue beating for 1 minute at a time until the correct temperature is reached.

8. Add the eggs one at a time, beating at a medium speed until fully incorporated before adding the next egg. Once all the eggs are in, stop the mixer, scrape down the sides, and beat on a medium speed for another 5 to 10 seconds until fully mixed.

9. Preheat the oven to 190°C, and line a baking tray with baking paper.

10. Transfer the choux batter to a large piping bag fitted with a large star tip. To keep the baking paper from moving as you work, pipe a small blob of choux pastry under all four corners of the baking paper.

11. Pipe ten to twelve 10-by-3½-cm logs on to the baking paper. Bake for 40 minutes, until the éclairs are a deep golden brown and well puffed. Turn off the oven and prop open the door with a wooden spoon, allowing the éclairs to sit for another 20 to 30 minutes in the warm oven. Transfer the éclairs to a wire rack to cool completely.

To make the icing:

12. Stir together the espresso powder with very hot water in a small bowl. Set aside.

13. Whisk together the icing sugar, corn syrup, vanilla and 3 tablespoons of double cream in a small bowl until smooth. If the mixture is too thick, add 1 additional teaspoon of double cream at a time until the desired consistency is reached.

14. Pour half of the icing into a separate small bowl. Stir in the espresso mixture until it's fully mixed. Transfer both icings to separate piping bags, both fitted with flat tips.

To assemble:

15. Whisk the chilled mocha crème pâtissière until smooth, then transfer it to a piping bag fitted with a filling tip. Insert the tip into one end of the éclair and pipe the filling in until you can just feel the éclair begin to expand. Be careful not to overfill, or the éclairs may split – work slowly and carefully. If necessary, insert the tip into the opposite end to finish filling the éclair.

16. Repeat this process until all the éclairs are filled. Pipe the vanilla icing over the éclairs, then pipe three zigzag stripes across the width of each éclair with the espresso icing. Let the icing set for 20 to 30 minutes (if you can wait that long) before serving. Keep chilled and serve cold.

note: If your icing has a thin enough consistency, you can also drag a toothpick along the length of the éclairs while the icing is still wet, moving in the direction of the zigzag points, to create a more feathered pattern.

Taillow
Chocolate Cherry Olive Oil Cake

It's easy for flavours to get lost in chocolate cakes, but the cherries in this olive oil cake hold their own against the dark chocolate. Instead of getting overwhelmed by chocolatey goodness, they stand out, like a courageous and defiant Taillow, adding bursts of tart flavour and rich red colour.

Difficulty: ● ○ ○ ○
Prep time: 15 minutes
Bake time: 50 minutes
Yield: Serves 12 to 16
Dietary notes: Vegetarian

Equipment: 20-cm round cake tin, food mixer, wire cooling rack, microwave

60 ml olive oil
120 ml tart cherry juice
165 g light brown sugar
½ teaspoon salt
110 g dark chocolate, melted and cooled
2 large eggs
1 tablespoon vanilla extract
1 teaspoon almond extract
120 g plain flour
60 g cocoa powder
½ teaspoon bicarbonate of soda
140 g dried cherries
Dark chocolate
White chocolate
Red candy melts

1. Preheat the oven to 165°C. Grease a 20-cm cake tin and line the bottom with a circle of baking paper. Grease the baking paper.

2. Beat the olive oil, cherry juice, brown sugar and salt together in a food mixer fitted with a paddle attachment until combined. Add the chocolate and mix to combine. Add the eggs, one at a time, beating until fully incorporated before adding the next egg. Mix in the vanilla and almond extracts.

3. Mixing on a low speed, add the flour, cocoa powder and bicarbonate of soda, mixing until just combined. Fold in the dried cherries. Pour the batter into the prepared cake tin and bake for 45 to 50 minutes or until a cake tester inserted into the centre of the cake comes out with just a few moist crumbs on it.

4. Let the cake cool in the tin for 15 minutes before turning it out and flipping it on to a wire rack to cool completely.

5. Add the dark chocolate to a microwave-safe bowl and microwave in 30-second bursts, stirring each time, until the chocolate is melted and smooth. Repeat this process with the white chocolate and red candy melts.

6. Drizzle the dark chocolate, white chocolate and red candy melts all over the cooled cake. Cut and serve at room temperature.

Whismur
Lemon-Lavender Bars

Whismur may look cute and unassuming, but it can let out an ear-splitting scream at a moment's notice. Likewise, these lemon-lavender bars look sweet and simple with a cute lavender icing on top, but that lemon hiding underneath might make you pucker!

Difficulty: ● ● ○ ○
Prep time: 30 minutes
Bake time: 1 hour
Rest time: 1½ hours
Chill time: 1 hour
Yield: 24 bars
Dietary notes: Vegetarian

Equipment: 22-by-33-cm baking tin, food processor, medium saucier, small saucepan, offset spatula

Crust

120 g plain flour
100 g icing sugar
½ teaspoon salt
1½ teaspoons culinary lavender
120 g unsalted butter, cubed

Lemon Curd

300 g sugar
1 tablespoon cornflour
240 ml lemon juice
3 large eggs
4 large egg yolks
60 g unsalted butter

Lavender Icing

3 tablespoons whole milk
2 teaspoons culinary lavender
1 drop red food colouring (optional)
3 to 4 drops blue food colouring (optional)
100 g sugar
Black gel icing

To make the crust:

1. Preheat the oven to 165°C. Grease a 22-by-33-cm baking tin, then line it with baking paper so that there is a 5-cm overhang of baking paper on the long edges.

2. Add the flour, icing sugar, salt, lavender and butter to the bowl of a food processor. Pulse until combined and the mixture resembles wet sand.

3. Press the crust into the bottom of the prepared tin and up the sides by about 1 cm. Use the flat bottom of a glass or cup to really compress the crust. Bake for 30 minutes until the crust is just beginning to turn golden. Remove from the oven and set aside.

To make the lemon curd:

4. Whisk together the sugar and cornflour in a medium saucier to combine, then add the lemon juice, eggs and egg yolks, whisking to combine. Place the saucier over a medium heat and continue whisking gently and constantly until the mixture comes to a boil, about 5 to 7 minutes. Once it starts boiling, continue cooking and whisking for about 30 seconds before removing it from the heat. Stir in the butter until it's melted and smooth.

note: Sauciers have curved bottoms, which makes them preferable when a mixture will likely get trapped in the edges of a straight-sided saucepan. A saucepan is okay to use if you don't have a saucier, but you'll have to be extra vigilant and thorough with stirring so that the mixture doesn't get trapped in the edges and burn.

5. Pour the lemon curd on to the prepared crust, then return the tin to a 165°C oven and bake for an additional 15 to 20 minutes until the filling is set. Remove the tin from the oven and leave to cool for 1 hour before moving it to the fridge to chill completely.

continued on the next page

To make the lavender icing:

6. Make the icing as the lemon bars cool. Bring the milk and lavender to a boil in a small saucepan over a high heat. Remove from heat, cover and leave to sit for at least 30 minutes. Strain into a bowl and discard the lavender.

7. Place the icing sugar in a medium bowl. Stir the lavender-infused milk together with the food colouring (if using), then stir it into the icing sugar until smooth. Pour the icing over the chilled lemon bars, spreading in an even layer with an offset spatula. Let the bars set, uncovered, in the fridge for 1 hour.

8. Use the overhanging baking paper to carefully lift the lemon bars out of the baking tin and transfer them to a chopping board. Use a sharp knife to cut them into 24 bars. Decorate each bar with 2 "+" symbols made up of four lines using black gel icing. Keep chilled and serve cold.

> **note:** Creating a sling with baking paper or aluminum foil is always a good idea. It makes removing your bakes from their vessels much easier and can help prevent breakage.

Spoink
Black Sesame Cream Puffs

The pink pearl on Spoink's head amplifies its psychokinetic powers. The raspberry on top of this sesame custard–filled cream puff adds a splash of colour and bright tartness to these sweet treats, and that's almost as good! Although the sesame paste used in this recipe is deep, dark black, it turns a soft grey, just like Spoink, when mixed into the custard.

Difficulty: ● ● ● ○
Prep time: 20 minutes
Bake time: 30 minutes
Rest time: 50 minutes
Chill time: 4 hours
Yield: 12 cream puffs
Dietary notes: Vegetarian

Equipment: Medium saucepan, fine mesh sieve, medium saucier, instant-read thermometer, food mixer, baking tray, two piping bags with large and 1-cm round tips, wire cooling rack

Black Sesame Crème Pâtissière
360 ml whole milk
120 ml double cream
100 g sugar
3 tablespoons cornflour
4 large egg yolks
2 tablespoons black sesame paste

Choux Pastry
240 ml whole milk
90 g unsalted butter
1 tablespoon sugar
¾ teaspoon salt
120 g plain flour, sifted
4 large eggs

Topping
12 maraschino cherries

To make the black sesame crème pâtissière:

1. Bring the milk and double cream to a bare simmer in a medium saucepan over a medium heat, stirring occasionally. Remove from heat.

2. Whisk together the sugar and cornflour. Add the egg yolks and whisk until smooth. While whisking constantly, slowly pour the hot milk and cream mixture into the cornflour mixture.

3. Pour this mixture back into the saucepan and return it to a medium heat. Whisk constantly until the mixture begins to bubble. The moment you see it bubble, set a 1-minute timer and continue to whisk constantly. Remove from heat.

4. Add the black sesame paste to a medium bowl, then set a fine mesh sieve over the bowl. Pour the crème pâtissière through the fine mesh sieve, pushing it through with a plastic spatula. Let it sit for 3 to 5 minutes to allow the black sesame paste to soften, then stir until smooth. Leave the crème pâtissière to cool for 20 minutes at room temperature before covering and chilling for at least 4 hours.

> **note:** Sauciers have curved bottoms, which makes them preferable when a mixture will likely get trapped in the edges of a straight-sided saucepan. A saucepan is okay to use if you don't have a saucier, but you'll have to be extra vigilant and thorough with stirring so that the mixture doesn't get trapped in the edges and burn.

To make the choux pastry:

5. While the crème pâtissière chills, make the cream puff shells. Bring the milk, butter, sugar and salt to the boil in a medium saucier over a high heat. Remove from heat and vigorously stir in the flour with a wooden spoon until smooth.

6. Return the saucier to a high heat and continue stirring vigorously until an instant-read thermometer registers 75°C when inserted into the mixture.

continued on the next page

7. Tip the mixture into the bowl of a food mixer fitted with a paddle attachment. Beat on a medium speed until the temperature drops to 60°C or lower. Start taking the temperature after about 3 minutes, then continue beating for 1 minute at a time until the correct temperature is reached.

8. Add the eggs one at a time, beating at a medium speed until fully incorporated before adding the next egg. Once all the eggs are in, stop the mixer, scrape down the sides, and beat on a medium speed for another 5 to 10 seconds until fully mixed.

9. Preheat the oven to 200°C, and line a baking tray with baking paper.

10. Transfer the choux batter to a large piping bag fitted with a large round tip. To keep the baking paper from moving as you work, pipe a small blob of choux pastry under all four corners of the baking paper.

11. Pipe 12 equal mounds on to the baking paper. Use a wet finger to smooth the tops of each mound. Bake for 30 minutes, until the mounds are a deep golden brown and well puffed. Turn off the oven and prop open the door with a wooden spoon, allowing the cream puffs to sit for another 30 minutes in the warm oven. Transfer them to a wire rack to cool completely.

To assemble:

12. Whisk the chilled black sesame crème pâtissière until smooth, then transfer it to a piping bag fitted with a round tip. Use a serrated knife to carefully saw off the tops of the cream puffs to reveal a 2½-cm hole. Pipe the black sesame crème pâtissière into the cream puff, filling the entire pastry; continue piping until a rounded mound stands about 2½ cm over the top of the cream puff.

13. Repeat this process until all the cream puffs are filled. Top each one with a maraschino cherry.

Flygon
Pan Pizza

Flygon's wings are so powerful that they can create sandstorms – here, we cut the basil into wing shapes to deliver a powerful herb-y flavour. With the bursts of red and green from the sauce and basil, and with the olives adding a pleasant earthy note for this Ground-type Pokémon, you might burst into song when you try it, just like the music-like sound you hear when Flygon, the Desert Spirit, flaps its wings.

Difficulty: ● ● ○ ○
Prep time: 20 minutes
Rest time: 2 hours
Bake time: 15 minutes
Yield: 8 slices
Dietary notes: Vegetarian

Equipment: Food mixer, 25- or 30-cm cast-iron pan

Dough
300 g strong white bread flour
1½ teaspoons salt
2 teaspoons instant yeast
3 tablespoons olive oil, plus more for the pan
180 ml lukewarm water

Toppings
180 ml passata
225 g grated mozzarella
Kalamata olives
Fresh basil

1. Add the flour, salt, yeast and olive oil to the bowl of a food mixer fitted with a dough hook attachment. Mix on a low speed to combine, then slowly drizzle in the water. Once a shaggy dough forms (the dough will be lumpy, with no dry flour remaining), increase the speed to medium and knead for 10 to 15 minutes until the dough is smooth and elastic.

2. Pour 2 to 3 tablespoons olive oil into a 30-cm cast-iron pan, tilting the pan to coat the sides and bottom of the pan. You can also use a 25-cm pan, but the dough will be thicker and require more baking time.

3. Transfer the dough to the pan, stretching and pressing the dough towards the edges of the pan. Don't force the dough: Just get it as flat and wide as you can without tearing it – the dough will relax and spread as it rises. Cover the dough and let it rise until it's puffy and has doubled in volume, about 2 hours.

4. For the last 30 minutes of rising time, move one of your oven racks to the lowest position, then preheat the oven to 260°C.

5. Gently stretch the risen dough to the edges of the pan, taking care not to deflate it too much. Spoon the marinara sauce over the top of the dough, spreading it all the way to the edges in an even layer.

6. Scatter the shredded mozzarella over the top of the pizza, all the way to the edges. Top with halved kalamata olives. Bake for 15 minutes or until the top is golden and bubbling. Carefully lift one of the edges of the pizza with a thin metal spatula to check the bottom – it should be golden brown. If it's not golden brown but the top is done, heat the skillet on the hob over a medium flame until the crust is the right colour.

7. Trim the basil leaves into kite shapes (like Flygon's wings!). Scatter over the top of the hot pizza, slice it into 8 equal slices, and serve.

Sinnoh Region

Bidoof Peanut Butter
Pretzel Tart

Combee Honey Cake

Kricketot Chocolate
Strawberry Sandwich Cookies

Drifloon Blackberry Galette

Gastrodon Cheesecake Swirl
Bars with Chocolate Streusel

Buizel Apricot
Thumbprint Cookies

Bidoof
Peanut Butter Pretzel Tart

Bidoof will gnaw on just about anything, from logs and rocks to people's houses. This peanut butter tart won't help a Bidoof hone its big front teeth, but it tastes an awful lot better than rocks and logs. The malty, salty pretzel crust pairs beautifully with the sweetened peanut butter filling and rich chocolate ganache, creating a rich tart and a crunchy, satisfying tribute to the imperturbable Plump Mouse Pokémon.

Difficulty: ● ● ○ ○
Prep time: 20 minutes
Bake time: 15 minutes
Chill time: 4 hours
Yield: Serves 8 to 12
Dietary notes: Vegetarian

Equipment: Food processor, 22-cm tart tin with removable bottom, wire cooling rack, food mixer, hand mixer, offset spatula, three piping bags (one with large round tip and one with fine writing tip), microwave

Crust
225 g pretzels
3 tablespoons light brown sugar
90 g unsalted butter, melted

Filling
225 g cream cheese
55 g light brown sugar
1 cup smooth peanut butter
110 g icing sugar
240 ml cream, plus 3 tablespoons for assembling

Decorations
90 g dark chocolate, chopped
30 g white chocolate
1 maraschino cherry

To make the crust:

1. Preheat the oven to 180°C. Add the pretzels and brown sugar to the bowl of a food processor. Pulse until finely ground. Transfer to a medium bowl.

2. Stir the butter into the pretzel mixture until fully incorporated. Press the mixture into the bottom and all the way up the sides of a 22-cm tart tin with a removable bottom. Use the smooth bottom of a glass or cup to fully compact the crust.

3. Bake the crust for 15 minutes until slightly darkened and set. Allow to cool completely on a wire cooling rack.

To make the filling:

4. Beat the cream cheese, brown sugar and peanut butter in the bowl of a food mixer fitted with a paddle attachment at a medium speed until light, fluffy and smooth. Reduce the speed to low, then add the icing sugar. Beat until combined, then increase the speed to medium-high, beating until light, fluffy and smooth, about 8 to 10 minutes.

5. Add 240 ml of the double cream to a large bowl. Beat with a hand mixer until soft peaks form, about 5 minutes. Carefully fold the whipped cream into the peanut butter mixture.

6. Spoon the mixture into the cooled tart shell, smoothing and levelling the filling with an offset spatula. Reserve about 1 cup of the filling.

7. Spoon the remaining filling into a piping bag fitted with a large round tip. Pipe the filling into puffy swoops all along the outer edge of the tart, just like Bidoof's fluffy cheeks.

8. Add the dark chocolate and 3 tablespoons of double cream to a small bowl. Microwave for 1 minute and stir until smooth. If solid bits of chocolate remain, microwave for an additional 15 seconds at a time until fully melted and smooth. Let the ganache cool slightly.

continued on the next page

9. As the ganache cools, add the white chocolate to a microwave-safe bowl and microwave in bursts of 30 seconds, stirring each time, until melted and smooth. Transfer the white chocolate to a small piping bag and snip off the end.

To decorate:

10. Transfer the chocolate ganache to a piping bag fitted with a fine writing tip. Pipe an outline of Bidoof's eyes and muzzle. Pipe a large square of white chocolate in the lower centre of the muzzle to form Bidoof's teeth.

11. Fill in the muzzle with the chocolate ganache. Pipe two small dots for Bidoof's eyes. After a few minutes, if the eyes are set, pipe two smaller white dots on top to finish the eyes. (If the ganache isn't set, chill for 5 to 10 minutes before piping the white chocolate on.) Pipe a thin outline around the teeth, plus one line straight up the middle to separate them into two teeth. Drizzle any remaining ganache in decorative swirls all over the fluffy mounds of filling you piped earlier. Halve the maraschino cherry, and place one half in the centre of the muzzle to form Bidoof's nose. (Feel free to snack on the other half of the cherry!) The filling should be cold enough to set the ganache as you work – if not, chill for 20 additional minutes before slicing and serving.

Combee
Honey Cake

Combee are one of the hardest-working Pokémon, spending their days gathering nectar. Both this cake and its frosting are just as sweet as the nectar Combee collects, and when you share this delicate honey cake with dear friends, you'll feel as close as the hundreds of Combee who sleep packed together in a drowsy, satisfied clump.

Difficulty: ● ○ ○ ○
Prep time: 15 minutes
Bake time: 50 minutes
Yield: Serves 8 to 12
Dietary notes: Vegetarian

Equipment: 20-cm cake tin, food mixer, wire cooling rack, hand mixer, offset spatula, microwave, piping bags with flat nozzle and fine writing tip

Cake
120 g unsalted butter, room temperature
100 g sugar
170 g honey
2 large eggs
1 teaspoon vanilla extract
120 ml whole milk
200 g plain flour
1¼ teaspoons baking powder
½ teaspoon bicarbonate of soda
½ teaspoon salt

Frosting
90 g unsalted butter
110 g honey
200 g icing sugar
¼ teaspoon salt
1 tablespoon lemon juice
Red food colouring
Yellow food colouring

Decorations
30 g dark chocolate chips

To make the cake:

1. Preheat the oven to 180°C. Grease a 20-cm cake tin and line the bottom with a circle of baking paper. Grease the baking paper.

2. Add the butter, sugar and honey to the bowl of a stand mixer fitted with a paddle attachment. Cream together at a medium speed until light and fluffy, about 5 to 7 minutes. Beat in the eggs, one at a time, allowing each egg to fully incorporate.

3. Beat in the vanilla and milk. Reduce the mixer speed to low, then add the flour, baking powder, bicarbonate of soda and salt, mixing until just incorporated. Scrape down the sides and bottom of the bowl with a plastic spatula to ensure that the batter is fully mixed.

4. Scrape the batter into the prepared tin, smoothing the top with a plastic spatula. Bake for 45 to 50 minutes, until a cake tester or toothpick inserted into the centre of the cake comes out with just a few moist crumbs. Let the cake cool in the tin for 20 minutes before transferring it to a wire rack to cool completely.

To make the frosting:

5. Using a hand mixer, beat together the butter, honey, icing sugar, salt and lemon juice in a large bowl until smooth, about 8 to 10 minutes.

6. Remove 2 tablespoons of frosting and transfer to a clean small bowl. Add 1 to 2 drops of red food colouring and 4 to 6 drops of yellow food colouring to make orange frosting. Beat until uniform in colour, about 1 minute. Remove 1 teaspoon of the original, uncoloured frosting and transfer to a small bowl. Add 4 to 6 drops of red food colouring and stir with a spoon until uniform in colour to make red frosting. (If you want your uncoloured base frosting to be yellower, add a few drops of yellow food colouring until it matches Combee.)

continued on the next page

To decorate:

7. If the cake is quite domed, trim off the rounded top of the cake with a serrated knife to level it. Draw a Combee template of all three Combee hexagons together on a 20-cm round of baking paper – the Combee will be about 18 cm wide at its widest and 18 cm tall from the top of the upper hexagon to the bottom of the lower hexagon. Cut the template out and place it on top of the cake. Use a sharp knife to cut the cake into Combee's shape using the template as your guide. (Snack on the trimmings while you decorate!)

8. Spread the yellow base frosting evenly over the top and sides of the cake with an offset spatula. Add the orange frosting to a small piping bag fitted with a flat nozzle. Pipe the frosting into three hexagonal shapes to create the outline around the faces on Combee. Dip your finger in water and use it to smooth out any rough spots or overlaps. Use a small offset spatula to create the small red wedge shape on the lower face, or pipe it with another flat nozzle and smooth it with the spatula or your finger.

9. Heat the chocolate chips in a microwave-safe bowl on high for 30-second bursts, stirring each time, until melted and smooth. Leave to cool slightly, then transfer to a piping bag with a fine writing tip. Pipe two eyes and a smiling mouth on to each of the three faces. Pipe two antennae (about 5 to 7 cm long) on to a baking tray lined with baking paper. Chill until completely set, about 10 to 15 minutes, then insert into the top corner of the top two faces.

note: Unable to make a template? Try these steps with your round cake: Cut a short but wide "v" out of the top of the cake. From each side of the "v," cut down horizontally towards the sides of the cake at a similar angle. Cut straight down, then cut horizontally down into the cake, at the same angle as the cut above. Cut straight down from there, then cut horizontally down towards the bottom of the cake to create the bottom point. Repeat on the other side of the cake, mirroring your work as much as possible. Aim for each edge being as straight and equal in length to all the other sides.

Kricketot
Chocolate Strawberry Sandwich Cookies

Kricketot are musical in nature – they make xylophone sounds by clanging their antennae together. The cookies and filling are similar to Kricketot's colouring, so use whatever shape you have on hand but if you can find a cutter shaped like a musical note, it would make the cookies extra special!

Difficulty: ● ○ ○ ○
Prep time: 15 minutes
Chill time: 1 hour
Bake time: 14 minutes
Yield: About 12 sandwich cookies
Dietary notes: Vegetarian

Equipment: Food processor, 2 baking trays, cookie cutters, wire cooling rack

150 g plain flour
40 g cocoa powder
120 g unsalted butter, softened
100 g sugar
½ teaspoon salt
1 large egg
Strawberry jam

1. Add the flour, cocoa powder, butter, sugar and salt to the bowl of a food processor. Pulse until combined. Add the egg to the mixture and pulse until a soft dough forms.

2. Sandwich the dough between two sheets of baking paper. Roll out to a thickness of ¼ cm. Transfer to a baking tray, then freeze for 1 hour.

3. Preheat the oven to 180°C.

4. Remove the top layer of baking paper from the cookie dough. Cut out as many cookies in your chosen shape as you can. Gather up the scraps, sandwich them between the two sheets of baking paper, roll out the dough, and cut out more cookies, repeating the process until you can no longer make more cookies.

5. Transfer the cookies to a baking paper-lined baking tray. Leave about 1 cm between the cookies – they won't spread very much, if at all.

6. Bake the cookies for 12 to 14 minutes, or until set. Let them cool for 5 minutes in the tray, then transfer them to a wire rack to cool completely.

7. Spread a thin layer of strawberry jam on to the flat side of a cookie, then sandwich with a second cookie. Repeat until you've used up all the cookies.

Drifloon
Blackberry Galette

Eek! Did you know that sometimes when children hang on to a Drifloon, they disappear? Well, after taking just one bite of this blackberry galette, the only thing at risk of disappearing is the rest of the galette. Packed with luscious blackberries, the filling in this galette is a deep purple, reminiscent of Drifloon, and the whipped cream looks just like the fluff on Drifloon's head!

Difficulty: ● ● ○ ○
Prep time: 20 minutes
Chill time: 1 hour
Bake time: 35 minutes
Yield: Serves 8
Dietary notes: Vegetarian

Equipment: Food processor, baking tray, wire cooling rack, hand mixer

Crust
120 g plain flour
60 g rye flour
120 g unsalted butter, cubed
½ teaspoon salt
1 tablespoon sugar
1 large egg
2 tablespoons double cream

Filling
500 g blackberries
150 g sugar
Zest and juice of 1 lemon
3 tablespoons cornflour

To Assemble and Serve
1 large egg
Yellow decorative sugar
Demerara sugar
1 cup double cream
2 tablespoons icing sugar

note: Rye flour adds a nutty flavour and a crunchier texture to the galette crust, but you can substitute additional plain flour if rye flour is unavailable.

1. Add the flour, rye flour, butter, salt and sugar to the bowl of a food processor. Pulse until the mixture resembles wet sand. Add 1 egg and 2 tablespoons double cream and process until the dough forms. Shape into a disc, wrap tightly in cling film, and chill for 1 hour.

2. For the filling, combine the blackberries, sugar, lemon zest and juice and cornflour in a large bowl. Toss to evenly coat.

3. Preheat the oven to 220°C. Line a baking tray with baking paper.

4. Place the chilled dough on to a floured work surface. Remove about 2 tablespoons of dough and set aside. Roll out the remaining dough to a thickness of about ½ cm, then transfer it to the prepared baking tray.

5. To assemble, spoon the filling into the centre of the crust, leaving a border of about 5 cm. Fold the edges of the crust towards the centre, pleating every few centimetres or so.

6. Shape the 2 tablespoons of dough you set aside into an x shape at an angle. Place on the same tray as the galette.

7. Beat the egg together with 1 tablespoon water. Brush the crust of the galette and the + with the egg wash. Coat the + shape in yellow sugar and sprinkle demerara sugar on the crust of the galette.

8. Transfer the baking tray to the oven, and bake for 35 minutes. About 10 to 12 minutes into the baking time, remove the + with a spatula and transfer it to a wire rack to cool.

9. Let the galette cool directly in the tray. Place the + at an angle on the exposed fruit in the centre of the cooled galette.

10. To serve, beat the double cream and icing sugar in a medium bowl with a hand mixer on a medium speed until medium peaks form. Slice and serve the galette with three dollops of whipped cream that look like the fluff on Drifloon's head.

Gastrodon

Cheesecake Swirl Bars with Chocolate Streusel

Gastrodon can be blue or pink, depending on if it comes from the western side or eastern side of Sinnoh. With this recipe, you can choose a raspberry swirl for an East Sea look, or a blueberry swirl for a West Sea look. The streusel topping evokes Gastrodon's plate, a remnant from the huge protective shell it had in ancient times.

Difficulty: ● ● ○ ○
Prep time: 20 minutes
Bake time: 1 hour
Chill time: 4 hours
Yield: 24 bars
Dietary notes: Vegetarian

Equipment: 22-by-33-cm baking tray, food processor, hand mixer, medium saucepan, blender, fine mesh sieve

Crust
450 g digestive biscuits
2 tablespoons light brown sugar
½ teaspoon salt
60 g unsalted butter, melted

Filling
Three 225 g tubs cream cheese, softened
120 ml sour cream, room temperature
200 g sugar
1 tablespoon vanilla paste or extract
3 large eggs, room temperature

Fruit Swirl
340 g frozen raspberries or blueberries
50 g sugar
Zest and juice of 1 lemon

Chocolate Streusel Topping
90 g plain flour
40 g cocoa powder
55 g light brown sugar
¼ teaspoon salt
75 g butter, melted

To make the crust:

1. Preheat the oven to 180°C. Grease a 22-by-33-cm baking tray, then line the tray with baking paper so there is a 5-cm overhang on the long sides of the tray.

2. Add the digestive biscuits, brown sugar and salt to the bowl of a food processor. Pulse until finely ground. Tip the contents into a large bowl, then pour in the butter. Stir until no dry crumbs remain.

3. Press the crust mixture into the bottom of the prepared tray, using the flat bottom of a glass or cup to tightly pack the crust. Bake for about 20 minutes, until the crust is set and just beginning to darken. Set aside and leave to cool while you make the filling.

To make the filling:

4. Add the cream cheese, sour cream and sugar to a large bowl. Beat together with a hand mixer until light and fluffy. Add the vanilla and mix to combine. Add the eggs one at a time, beating until each egg is fully incorporated before adding the next one.

5. Pour the filling on to the prepared crust and set aside while you make the fruit swirl.

note: Instead of choosing between blue or pink, you can do both! Use 170 g of frozen raspberries and 170 g of frozen blueberries to create a real West Sea and East Sea experience. Combine each type of berry with half the sugar and half the lemon juice and zest, following the purée instructions in step 6 one at a time, then spoon each purée over half of the filling and carefully swirl each half without intermixing them in step 8. To be true to nature, serve the blueberry bars on the left for the West Sea and the raspberry bars on the right for the East Sea!

To make the fruit swirl:

6. Add the berries, sugar and lemon zest and juice to a medium saucepan. Cook over a medium heat, stirring occasionally, until the berries begin to break down, release their juices and start to bubble. Leave to cool, then transfer the berries to a blender. Blend until smooth, then pour the fruit purée through a fine mesh sieve into a bowl. Discard the solids, and let the strained purée cool while you make the streusel topping.

To make the chocolate streusel topping and finish:

7. Whisk together the flour, cocoa powder, brown sugar and salt in a small bowl until combined. Stir in the butter until a wet, crumbly mixture forms.

8. Spoon the fruit purée over the cheesecake filling. Gently swirl a butter knife through the cheesecake filling to create a marbled effect, but be careful not to overmix. Sprinkle the streusel topping over the top of the cheesecake.

9. Bake for 35 to 40 minutes until set. The cheesecake will be a bit wobbly in the centre, but it shouldn't be totally liquid. Leave to cool at room temperature for 1 hour, then move to the fridge to chill for at least 4 hours. Cut into 24 squares, then serve.

Apricot Thumbprint Cookies

These cookies emulate the shape of Buizel's collar, which it uses as a floatation device, with an orange-coloured, apricot-flavoured centre. We tame the sweetness of the cookie and filling with some dark chocolate whiskers that give each cookie extra depth – and, of course, cuteness.

Difficulty: ● ○ ○ ○
Prep time: 15 minutes
Bake time: 15 minutes
Yield: 18 cookies
Dietary notes: Vegetarian

Equipment: Two baking trays, hand mixer, wire cooling racks, microwave, piping bag with fine writing tip

180 g plain flour
50 g almond flour
150 g unsalted butter, softened
130 g sugar
1 large egg
2 teaspoons vanilla extract
½ teaspoon almond extract
110 g apricot jam
Dark chocolate, chopped

1. Preheat the oven to 180°C. Line two baking trays with baking paper.

2. Whisk together the flour and almond flour in a large bowl. Add the butter and sugar, then beat together with a hand mixer until combined. Beat in the egg, followed by the vanilla and almond extracts.

3. Scoop 9 walnut-size balls of cookie dough on to one of the prepared baking trays. Repeat with the remaining dough and baking tray. Use your thumb to make a divot in each cookie. Spoon about ½ teaspoon of jam into each divot.

4. Bake for about 15 minutes, until the cookies are set and just turning golden brown around the edges. Cool in the tray for 10 minutes before transferring the cookies to a wire rack to cool completely.

5. When the cookies are cool, add the chopped dark chocolate to a microwave-safe bowl. Microwave in 30-second bursts, stirring each time, until the chocolate is melted and smooth. Spoon into a small piping bag fitted with a fine writing tip.

6. Pipe a nose in the centre of the jam, then pipe two sets of whiskers on opposite sides of each cookie to match Buizel's face.

Unova Region

Snivy Lemon Biscotti with Chocolate, Pistachios & Candied Lemon Peel

Tepig Spiced Chocolate Bundt Cake

Oshawott Blueberry Meringue Tartlets

Sandile Butterscotch & Brownie Parfait

Scraggy Orange Cardamom Sweet Rolls

Whimsicott Angel Food Cake

Snivy
Lemon Biscotti
with Chocolate, Pistachios & Candied Lemon Peel

Snivy uses its tail to get energy from sunlight, but humans get energy from rest and, of course, food! This crunchy biscotti is packed with bright lemony flavour, so every bite tastes a little like sunshine. Even the most discerning Snivy would approve. Serve with coffee or a tea of your choice for a calming afternoon snack – and stretch out in the sun for the fully Snivy experience.

Difficulty: ● ● ● ○
Prep time: 15 minutes
Bake time: 55 minutes
Yield: About 30 biscotti
Dietary notes: Vegetarian

Equipment: Baking tray, food mixer, wire cooling rack

120 g unsalted butter, softened
65 g sugar
65 g light brown sugar
½ teaspoon salt
1 tablespoon lemon zest
3 large eggs, divided
1 tablespoon vanilla
240 g plain flour
2 teaspoons baking powder
75 g chopped pistachios
60 g dark chocolate chips
40 g chopped candied lemon peel
Demerara sugar

1. Preheat the oven to 180°C. Line a baking tray with baking paper.

2. Beat together the butter, sugar, brown sugar, salt and lemon zest in the bowl of a food mixer fitted with a paddle attachment until light and fluffy, about 5 minutes. Beat in 2 eggs, along with the vanilla, on a medium speed until fully incorporated, about 2 to 3 minutes.

3. Reduce the mixer speed to low, then add the flour and baking powder. Mix until just about incorporated, then add the pistachios, chocolate chips and candied peel, mixing until evenly distributed.

4. Shape the dough into a flat, thick sheet that's about 38 cm long, 15 cm wide and 2½ cm tall. Place the dough on the prepared baking tray. Beat the remaining egg together with 1 tablespoon water. Brush the top of the log with a thin coating of egg wash, then sprinkle liberally with demerara sugar.

5. Bake the log for 30 to 35 minutes, until firm, and light golden brown. Let the biscotti log cool until you're able to handle it safely (note that it should still be warm, but not hot). Transfer to a chopping board, and carefully cut 1-cm slices crosswise from the log with a serrated knife, for a total of about 30 biscotti.

6. Transfer the cut biscotti back to the prepared baking tray, cut side up. They will not spread, so don't worry about leaving a lot of room between each one – 1 cm will do. Reduce the oven temperature to 165°C and bake for about 10 minutes, or until lightly browned.

7. Carefully flip over the biscotti, then bake for an additional 10 minutes, or until lightly browned. Let the biscotti cool in the tray for 5 minutes, then transfer them to a wire rack to cool completely.

Tepig
Spiced Chocolate Bundt Cake

This delicious chocolate cake gets a fiery kick from chilli powder mixed into the batter, as well as some warm aromatic cinnamon. When it's time to bake, stick with your trusty oven and don't depend on Tepig's fireballs. The cake is topped with spicy red cinnamon sweets shaped like the ball on Tepig's tail.

Difficulty: ● ● ○ ○
Prep time: 20 minutes
Bake time: 50 minutes
Yield: Serves 12 to 16
Dietary notes: Vegetarian

Equipment: 23-cm Bundt or cake ring tin, food mixer, wire cooling rack

Cake
120 g cocoa powder
2 teaspoons espresso powder
240 ml boiling water
240 ml buttermilk
225 g unsalted butter, melted
200 g sugar
220 g dark brown sugar
Zest of 1 orange
1 tablespoon vanilla extract
3 eggs, room temperature
360 g plain flour
1 teaspoon baking powder
½ teaspoon bicarbonate of soda
1 teaspoon salt
2 teaspoons ancho chilli powder
1 teaspoon cinnamon
¼ teaspoon cayenne

Icing
100 icing sugar
Zest of 1 orange
30 ml orange juice
15 ml double cream
1 drop red food colouring (optional)
6 to 8 drops yellow food colouring (optional)
Handful of small cinnamon sweets

1. Preheat the oven to 180°C. Grease a 23cm Bundt or cake ring tin.

2. Whisk together the cocoa powder, espresso powder and boiling water. Leave to sit for 2 minutes, then pour the liquid into the bowl of a food mixer fitted with a paddle attachment. Add the buttermilk, butter, sugar, dark brown sugar, orange zest and vanilla. Beat until smooth, about 5 minutes.

3. Add the eggs, one at a time, beating on a medium speed until fully incorporated before adding the next egg.

4. Whisk together the flour, baking powder, bicarbonate of soda, salt, ancho chilli powder, cinnamon and cayenne in a medium bowl. Reduce the mixer speed to low, and gradually add the flour mixture until it is fully combined. Scrape down the sides and bottom of the bowl to make sure the mixture is fully mixed.

5. Pour the batter into the prepared tin, smoothing the top of the batter with a plastic spatula. Bake for 45 to 50 minutes, until a cake tester inserted into the centre of the cake comes out clean. Let the cake cool in the tin for 30 minutes, before carefully inverting it on to a wire rack to cool completely.

6. Make the icing by beating together the icing sugar, orange zest, orange juice, double cream and red and yellow food colouring (if using) in a large bowl until smooth, about 8 to 10 minutes. Drizzle the icing over the top of the cooled cake, then scatter small cinnamon sweets over the icing.

Oshawott
Blueberry Meringue Tartlets

Oshawott sometimes uses the scalchop on its stomach to break open hard berries. The berries in this tart are soft and juicy, especially when topped with light, fluffy meringue and delicious chocolate details that reflect the adorable Sea Otter Pokémon!

Difficulty: ● ● ○ ○
Prep time: 30 minutes
Bake time: 30 minutes
Chill time: 1 hour and 10 minutes
Yield: 12 tartlets
Dietary notes: Vegetarian

Equipment: Food processor, 12-hole muffin tray or 12 fluted tartlet tins, 10-cm cookie cutter, food mixer or hand mixer, four piping bags (one with large round tip and three with fine writing tips), microwave, baking tray

Tart Shells

180 g plain flour
½ teaspoon salt
2 tablespoons sugar
120 g unsalted butter, cubed
2 to 3 tablespoons cold water

Filling

280 g blueberries, fresh or frozen
100 g sugar
1 tablespoon cornflour
Juice and zest of 1 lemon

To Assemble

12 blueberries
3 large egg whites
100 g sugar
White chocolate
Dark chocolate
Milk chocolate

To make the tart:

1. Add the flour, salt, sugar and butter to the bowl of a food processor. Pulse until the mixture resembles coarse sand. Add 2 tablespoons of water, and pulse until a smooth dough forms. If the dough is too dry, add 1 tablespoon of water, and pulse to combine.

2. Shape the dough into a disc, tightly wrap with cling film, and chill for at least 1 hour.

3. Meanwhile, add the blueberries, sugar, cornflour, lemon zest and lemon juice to a large bowl. Toss to combine, then lightly mash with a fork to break up some of the blueberries. No need to crush all of them – half or less is fine. Set aside.

4. Heat the oven to 200°C. Grease a standard muffin tray or 12 fluted tartlet tins. Place the chilled dough on to a floured work surface. Roll out to a thickness of about ¼ cm. Use a 10-cm round cookie cutter to cut out 12 circles of dough. If necessary, gather up and reroll the scraps to cut out additional circles.

5. Press the dough into the prepared muffin tray or tartlet tins. Give the blueberry filling a quick stir to redistribute, then spoon it into the tart shells, dividing evenly.

6. Bake for 25 to 30 minutes, until the tart shells are golden and the filling is bubbling. Leave the tartlets to cool completely in the tray before removing them, loosening the edges with a thin knife, if necessary.

To make the meringue:

7. Beat the egg whites on a medium speed in the bowl of a food mixer or using a handmixer, until thick and foamy. Continue beating while gradually adding the sugar. Increase the speed to medium-high and beat until stiff peaks form. Transfer the meringue to a piping bag fitted with a large round tip.

continued on the next page

To assemble:

8. Pipe a sphere of meringue on to each of the cooled tarts. Smooth the tops of the spheres with a wet finger. Place the blueberries on either side of the meringue to form Oshawott's ears. Chill, uncovered, in the fridge while you prepare the chocolate decorations.

9. Place the white, dark and milk chocolates into separate microwave-safe bowls. Microwave in bursts of 30 seconds, stirring each time, until all the chocolate is melted and smooth. Transfer the three chocolates into three separate piping bags fitted with fine writing tips.

10. Line a baking tray with baking paper. Pipe 24 dark chocolate circles to form Oshawott's eyes. Freeze for about 1 minute to set.

11. Pipe 24 white chocolate dots over the set dark chocolate to complete Oshawott's eyes. Pipe 72 tiny dots in dark chocolate to form the little spots on Oshawott's face, followed by 12 mouth shapes.

12. Pipe 12 milk chocolate spots to form Oshawott's nose. Chill to set for about 5 to 10 minutes.

13. Place 2 eyes, 1 nose, 1 mouth and 6 spots on each tart to form Oshawott's face. Keep chilled and serve cold.

Sandile
Butterscotch & Brownie Parfait

The layers of this parfait are inspired by Sandile's black and tan stripes. This dessert features pink raspberry whipped cream on the top – think of it as a Sandile flipped on its back asking for belly scratches. These parfaits are so tasty, they might just coax a Sandile or two out of their hiding spots deep in the sand.

Difficulty: ● ○ ○ ○
Prep time: 20 minutes
Bake time: 17 minutes
Chill time: 4 hours
Yield: 4 parfaits
Dietary notes: Vegetarian

Equipment: Medium saucepan, fine mesh sieve, baking tray, hand mixer

Butterscotch Crème Pâtissière
360 ml whole milk
120 ml double cream
100 g sugar
3 tablespoons cornflour
4 large egg yolks
1 teaspoon vanilla extract
90 g butterscotch chips

Crisp Brownie
100 g sugar
110 g light brown sugar
120 g unsalted butter, melted
60 g dark chocolate chips, melted
60 g dark cocoa powder
or regular cocoa powder
2 eggs
60 g plain flour
½ teaspoon salt

Raspberry Whipped Cream
240 ml double cream
25 g icing sugar
1 tablespoon raspberry powder,
or raspberry purée

1. Bring the milk and double cream to a bare simmer in a medium saucepan over a medium heat, stirring occasionally. Remove from heat.

2. Whisk together the sugar and cornflour. Add the egg yolks and whisk until smooth. While whisking constantly, slowly pour the milk and cream mixture into the cornflour mixture.

3. Pour this mixture back into the saucepan and return to a medium heat. Whisk constantly until the mixture begins to bubble. The moment you see it bubble, set a 1-minute timer and continue to whisk constantly. Remove from heat.

4. Add the vanilla and butterscotch chips to a medium bowl, then set a fine mesh sieve over the bowl. Pour the crème pâtissière through the fine mesh sieve, pushing it through with a plastic spatula. Leave to sit for 3 to 5 minutes to allow the butterscotch chips to melt, then stir until smooth. Leave to cool for 20 minutes at room temperature before covering and chilling for at least 4 hours.

5. Meanwhile, make the brownies. Preheat the oven to 165°C. Line a baking tray with baking paper, then grease the baking paper and sides of the tray.

6. Using a hand mixer, beat the sugar, brown sugar, butter, chocolate and dark cocoa together in a large bowl until smooth. Beat in the eggs. Add the flour and salt, stirring together until just combined.

7. Spread the brownie batter across the baking paper in a thin, even layer. It should just barely fill the tray. Bake for 15 to 17 minutes, until just set.

8. Leave the brownies to cool completely in the tray.

9. Whisk together the double cream, icing sugar and raspberry powder in a large bowl until soft peaks form, about 5 minutes.

10. Break apart the brownies using your hands – really get in there and break them into chunks and crumbs. Fill 4 glasses with alternating layers of crumbled brownies and butterscotch crème pâtissière before topping with a generous dollop of raspberry whipped cream. Keep chilled and serve cold.

Scraggy
Orange Cardamom Sweet Rolls

The rolls are shaped like Scraggy's head, complete with its signature smile in white chocolate, and the flavours are perfect for this dual-type Pokémon. Cardamom is an intense, smoky spice befitting a Dark-type Pokémon, and it's paired with punchy orange to jazz it up, like Scraggy's Fighting-type spirit!

Difficulty: ● ● ○ ○
Prep time: 20 minutes
Rest time: 2 hours
Bake time: 30 minutes
Yield: 12 rolls
Dietary notes: Vegetarian

Equipment: Food mixer, 22-by-33-cm baking tray, instant-read thermometer, small saucepan, wire cooling rack, microwave, two piping bags with fine writing tips

Rolls

1240 ml whole milk, lukewarm
110 g honey
2½ teaspoons active dry yeast
2 large eggs
480 g plain flour
½ teaspoon ground cardamom
1 teaspoon salt
60 g unsalted butter, softened
80 g chopped candied orange peel

Cardamom Syrup

50 g sugar
60 ml water
1 teaspoon ground cardamom

Decorations

Dried papaya
White chocolate
Dark chocolate

1. Stir together the milk, honey and yeast in the bowl of a food mixer fitted with a dough hook attachment. Leave to sit for 5 to 10 minutes, until foamy. (If the mixture doesn't foam, the milk may be too warm. The ideal temperature should be between 40°C and 45°C. If it still isn't foaming, your yeast may be dead, and you'll need to purchase new yeast.)

2. Add the eggs, flour, cardamom and salt. Mix on a low speed until a shaggy dough forms (the dough will be lumpy, with no dry flour remaining), then increase the speed to medium, mixing until the dough is smooth, about 10 minutes.

3. Add half the butter and continue kneading the dough until fully incorporated. Add the remaining butter and continue mixing for 15 minutes until the dough is smooth, slightly glossy and elastic.

4. Add the chopped candied orange peel and mix until evenly distributed. Cover the bowl and let the dough rise in a warm place for about 1 hour until it has puffed and doubled in size. While the dough rises, grease a 22-by-33-cm baking tray.

5. Gently punch down the dough to deflate, then turn it out on to a floured surface. Divide the dough into 12 equal portions.

6. Working with one piece of dough at a time, shape into a ball. Place the ball on the work surface and gently cup your hand over the dough ball, with your fingertips on the work surface. Rotate the dough to tighten the surface and shape it into a roll. Repeat with all the dough balls, then place them in the prepared baking tray, spacing them evenly. Lightly cover the balls with greased cling film. Leave them to rise for about 1 hour, until they're puffed and crowding the tray.

7. Towards the end of the rising time, preheat the oven to 180°C. When the rolls have risen, bake them for 25 to 30 minutes until they're golden brown and an instant-read thermometer registers 90°C when inserted into the centre of the rolls.

continued on the next page

8. While the rolls are baking, prepare the cardamom syrup. Add the sugar, water and cardamom to a small saucepan. Bring to the boil over a high heat, stirring occasionally until the sugar is dissolved. Remove from heat.

9. Brush the tops of the rolls with the syrup immediately after removing them from the oven. Let the rolls cool in the tray for 10 minutes before transferring them to a wire rack to cool down completely.

10. For the decorations, chop the dried papaya into thin sticks about 1½ cm tall. Insert the papaya into the top of each roll to create the small scale on top of Scraggy's head.

11. Add the white chocolate and dark chocolate to separate microwave-safe bowls. Heat both chocolates in the microwave in 30-second bursts until the chocolate is melted and smooth. Transfer the chocolates to separate piping bags fitted with fine writing tips.

12. Using the white chocolate, pipe 2 large circles on either side of each roll to create the white parts of Scraggy's eyes. Pipe 1 semicircle on the lower middle of each roll between the eyes to create Scraggy's mouth.

13. Pipe an outline around the large circles in dark chocolate. Use the dark chocolate to pipe an oblong circle in the centre of the white circles to finish Scraggy's eyes.

14. Pipe an outline around the semicircle using dark chocolate, then pipe two lines of dark chocolate on top of the semicircle to finish Scraggy's teeth. Pipe two small dots above the teeth to form Scraggy's nostrils.

Whimsicott
Angel Food Cake

Mischievous little Whimsicott loves to float around on whirlwinds, and this cake is light and fluffy to match! The delicate sweetness of the angel food cake is perfect for this Grass- and Fairy-type Pokémon and Whimsicott's cottony mane. But the addition of a lime curd creates a tart burst of lime on your tongue, like one of the surprising pranks Whimsicott loves to pull! The result is a cake that is sweet, surprising and bright.

Difficulty: ● ● ○ ○
Prep time: 30 minutes
Bake time: 45 minutes
Cool time: 3 hours
Yield: Serves 10 to 12
Dietary notes: Vegetarian

Equipment: 25-cm cake ring tin with feet, wire cooling rack, medium saucepan, hand mixer, two piping bags (one with a large round tip)

Cake

12 large egg whites
1 tablespoon lime juice
300 g sugar
1 tablespoon vanilla extract
150 g self-raising flour
½ teaspoon salt

Lime Curd

150 g sugar
2 teaspoons cornflour
120 ml lime juice
2 large eggs
2 large egg yolks
30 g unsalted butter
2 teaspoons matcha powder mixed with
1 tablespoon hot water until smooth
3 to 4 drops green food colouring
6 to 10 drops blue food colouring

Whipped Cream

480 ml double cream
25 g icing sugar

To make the cake:

1. Place an oven rack on the lower middle position. Preheat the oven to 165°C.

2. Add the egg whites and lime juice to the bowl of a food mixer fitted with a whisk attachment. Beat on a medium-low speed until frothy, about 1 minute. Increase the speed to medium-high, then very slowly add the sugar as it mixes. Continue beating until soft peaks form, about 5 minutes. Add the vanilla, beating until just combined.

3. Sift together the flour and salt. Add a quarter of the flour mixture to the egg white mixture. Gently fold in with a plastic spatula until fully incorporated. Repeat this process three more times, until all the flour mixture is incorporated.

4. Carefully pour the batter into an ungreased 25-cm cake ring tin with feet. Spread the batter evenly with a plastic spatula. Bake for 40 to 45 minutes, until a cake tester inserted into the centre of the cake comes out clean. Flip the tin cake side down and place it on a wire cooling rack to cool for 3 hours. Loosen the edges of the cake with a thin, sharp knife, then turn it back upside down. Tap the bottom of the tin until the cake releases.

To make the lime curd:

5. While the cake cools, make the lime curd. Whisk together the sugar and cornflour in a medium saucepan. Add the lime juice, eggs and egg yolks. Whisk until smooth, add the butter, then place the saucepan over a medium-low heat.

6. Cook, whisking gently but continuously, until thickened and beginning to bubble. When the first bubble appears, set a 1-minute timer and continue whisking. Remove from heat when the timer goes off. Add the matcha powder and food colouring, adjusting the levels of blue and green to match the green of Whimsicott's horns if necessary, and whisk until fully mixed.

7. Transfer the lime curd to a bowl, then cover it with cling film, pressing the plastic directly on to the surface of the curd to prevent a skin from forming on top. Chill for 1 hour.

continued on the next page

To make the whipped cream:

8. Make the whipped cream by adding the double cream and icing sugar to a large bowl. Whip with a hand mixer to form stiff peaks, about 7 minutes.

To decorate:

9. Spread the whipped cream over the entire surface of the cake, reserving about 1 cup of the whipped cream in a bowl.

10. Transfer the reserved whipped cream to a large piping bag. Trim off the tip of the piping bag to leave a 2½-cm opening. Pipe piles of whipped cream to mimic the fluff on top of Whimsicott's head and its beard on the upper and lower edges of the top of the cake.

11. Transfer the curd to a pastry bag fitted with a large round tip. Pipe on two large curls around the hole in the centre of the cake in the shape of Whimsicott's horns.

Kalos Region

Chespin Raspberry Pistachio Napoleon

Dedenne Mango-Gingerbread Pudding

Pyroar Spicy Pumpkin Empanadas

Tyrunt Chocolate Crinkle Cookies

Floette Focaccia

Chespin
Raspberry Pistachio Napoleon

The earthy brown pastry and pistachio cream in this bake reflect Chespin's colours. Puff pastry is normally baked to be light golden brown and puffy. In a Napoleon, you bake it a special way so that it ends up denser and darker brown – similar to how Chespin's soft quills can be flexed to become sharp and hard!

Difficulty: ● ● ○ ○
Prep time: 25 minutes
Bake time: 25 minutes
Chill time: 4 hours
Yield: Serves 6 to 8
Dietary notes: Vegetarian

Equipment: Two baking trays, pizza cutter, heavy oven-safe pan (such as cast iron), wire cooling rack, medium saucepan, fine mesh sieve, two piping bags (one with small star tip)

1 sheet frozen puff pastry, thawed
100 g sugar
3½ tablespoons cornflour
½ teaspoon salt
240 ml whole milk
240 ml double cream
90 g pistachio paste
30 g unsalted butter
4 to 6 drops green food colouring
Fresh raspberries
Icing sugar

note: If you can't find pistachio paste, you can make it! Bring a pan of water to the boil, then add 150 g of raw, shelled, whole pistachios and remove the pan from the heat. Leave to sit for 1 to 2 minutes, then drain. Pour the pistachios on to a clean kitchen towel and lightly rub them to gently peel off the skins. If any skins are stuck, remove them gently with your fingers.

In a food processer, add the cleaned pistachios and process for 2 to 4 minutes, until pasty. Add water (about 60 ml) and continue to process until smooth. This will make more than enough paste for this recipe – the rest can be stored in an airtight container for up to a week or frozen for up to 3 months.

1. Preheat the oven to 200°C. Line a baking tray with baking paper.

2. Use a pizza cutter or very sharp knife to cut the puff pastry into three equal rectangles. Place the pastry on the prepared baking tray, then place another sheet of baking paper on top of the pastry. Place the second baking tray on top of the baking paper-lined pastry, then weigh down the tray with a heavy oven-safe pan (a cast-iron pan works great here!).

3. Bake the pastry for 20 minutes. Remove the pan, the second baking tray, and the top layer of baking paper. If the pastry is deep golden brown all over, it's ready to go. If not, bake for an additional 5 minutes until uniformly browned. Leave the pastry to cool completely on a wire rack.

4. Whisk together the sugar, cornflour, and salt in a medium saucepan. Whisk in the milk and cream until smooth. Warm over a medium heat until the mixture begins to thicken and bubble, stirring constantly with a plastic spatula to keep it from scorching.

5. Place the pistachio paste and butter into a medium bowl. Set a fine mesh sieve over the top of the bowl, and pour the milk mixture through the sieve. Stir the pistachio cream until smooth. If using, add the green food colouring and stir until fully incorporated.

6. Cover the pistachio cream with cling film, pressing the plastic directly on to the surface of the cream (this prevents a skin from forming on top) and chill for 4 hours. After chilling, stir the cream until smooth, then scoop it into a piping bag fitted with a small star tip.

7. Lay one piece of the puff pastry on a serving plate. Alternate piping raspberry-sized rosettes of pistachio cream and placing raspberries on the puff pastry until it's completely covered. Carefully place a second piece of puff pastry on top. Repeat the alternating pattern of pistachio cream and raspberries until completely covered, reserving some of the pistachio cream. Top with the remaining piece of puff pastry.

8. Place a stiff card or piece of cardboard over part of the top of the pastry. Dust the top of the puff pastry with icing sugar, leaving the covered section free of sugar. Transfer any remaining pistachio cream to a piping bag. Trim the tip of the piping bag to leave a ½-cm opening. Pipe long quills clustered together on the sugar-free portion of the puff pastry in the pattern of Chespin's quills on top of its head. Keep chilled and serve cold.

Dedenne
Mango-Gingerbread Pudding

The big chocolate whiskers that decorate this bread pudding aren't capable of sending electric signals like Dedenne's whiskers. However, the mango nectar and the chunks of fresh mango give this pleasant dessert a bit of tang to zap your tongue. A perfect balance of sweet and tart for this Electric- and Fairy-type Pokémon.

Difficulty: ● ○ ○ ○
Prep time: 15 minutes
Bake time: 45 minutes
Chill time: 4 hours
Yield: Serves 12
Dietary notes: Vegetarian

Equipment: 22-by-33-cm baking tray, wire cooling racks, baking tray, microwave, piping bag with small round tip

240 ml whole milk
240 ml mango juice
120 ml double cream
4 large eggs
50 g sugar
2 teaspoons ground ginger
1 tablespoon vanilla extract
510 g chopped mango
680 g stale brioche, cubed
40 g chopped candied ginger
Dark chocolate
Dried papaya, cut into 5-cm rounds

1. Preheat the oven to 180°C. Grease a 22-by-33-cm baking tray.

2. Whisk together the milk, mango juice, double cream, eggs, sugar, ground ginger and vanilla in a very large bowl until smooth. Add the chopped mango, brioche and candied ginger, then gently fold and stir with a plastic spatula until evenly distributed and coated.

3. Pour the bread pudding mixture into the prepared baking tray. Bake for 45 minutes, until puffed, set and light golden brown on top. Leave to cool completely on a wire rack, then cover and transfer to the fridge to chill for 4 hours.

4. Line a baking tray with baking paper. When the bread pudding is cooled, add the dark chocolate to a microwave-safe bowl. Heat the chocolate in the microwave in 30-second bursts, stirring each time, until it's melted and smooth. Transfer the chocolate to a piping bag fitted with a small round tip.

5. Pipe a large pair of Dedenne's whiskers on to the baking paper. Chill in the freezer until completely set, about 5 minutes. While the chocolate chills, place the two papaya rounds on to the bread pudding to create Dedenne's cheek spots. Carefully remove the whiskers from the baking paper and transfer on to the cooled bread pudding, placing the inner corners of the whiskers on the centres of the cheek spots.

Pyroar
Spicy Pumpkin Empanadas

Bite into one of these empanadas and you'll see bursts of colour. Red from the peppers, orange from the pumpkin and black from the beans, all to match the colours of Pyroar's fur. The heat and smokiness from the chilli, paprika and cumin make these taste like they were baked over Pyroar's flames.

Difficulty: ● ● ○ ○
Prep time: 30 minutes
Chill time: 1 hour
Bake time: 20 minutes
Yield: 12 empanadas
Dietary notes: Vegetarian

Equipment: Food processor, large frying pan or cast-iron skillet, baking tray

Dough

240 g plain flour
½ teaspoon salt
120 g cold, unsalted butter, cubed
1 large egg
60 ml very cold water

Filling

1 tablespoon olive oil
½ medium onion, peeled and finely chopped
½ red pepper, diced
1 teaspoon salt
½ teaspoon black pepper
2 cloves garlic, chopped
½ red chilli, deseeded and chopped
½ teaspoon ground cumin
½ teaspoon smoked paprika
¼ teaspoon oregano
60 g tinned black beans, drained and rinsed
110 g pumpkin purée
60 g grated Edam cheese
1 large egg

1. Add the flour, salt and butter to the bowl of a food processor. Pulse until the mixture resembles wet sand. Add the egg and cold water, and pulse to form a smooth dough. Shape the dough into a disc, wrap tightly with cling film, and chill for 1 hour.

2. Make the filling while the dough chills. Heat the oil in a large frying pan or cast-iron skillet over a medium-high heat until shimmering. Add the onions and pepper, and season with salt and pepper. Cook, stirring frequently, until softened and beginning to brown around the edges, about 5 minutes. Add the garlic, chilli, cumin, paprika and oregano, and continue to cook until fragrant, about 30 seconds. Add the beans and pumpkin purée, stirring to combine. Remove from heat. Taste and add more salt and pepper, if needed. Set aside.

3. Preheat the oven to 200°C. Line a baking tray with baking paper.

4. Place the chilled dough on to a floured work surface. Roll to a thickness of about ¼ cm. Cut out six 15-cm circles using a small plate and sharp knife. Reroll the scraps and cut out more circles, repeating the process until you have 12 rounds.

5. Stir the grated cheese into the filling. Beat the egg together with 1 tablespoon of water. Scoop a small amount of filling into the centre of each round. Brush the edges of each round with the egg wash, then fold the rounds in half over the filling.

6. Crimp the edges of the empanadas to seal them. If you're not confident with your crimping abilities, don't worry: Use the prongs of a fork to press and seal the edges. Place the filled empanadas on the prepared baking tray and brush the tops with the remaining egg wash.

7. Bake for 20 minutes, until the empanadas are golden brown. Leave to cool for 10 minutes, then serve hot; alternatively, transfer to a wire rack to cool completely and serve at room temperature.

Tyrunt
Chocolate Crinkle Cookies

Crinkle cookies are kind of magical because they go into the oven as icing sugar–covered spheres, but they come out crinkled and craggy, sort of like the rocky hide on Tyrunt. Unlike a rock, though, these cookies are tender and chewy. Tyrunt love being pampered and hate sharing, but don't let them eat all your cookies!

Difficulty: ● ○ ○ ○
Prep time: 20 minutes
Chill time: 3 hours
Bake time: 26 minutes
Yield: About 18 cookies
Dietary notes: Vegetarian

Equipment: Food mixer, hand mixer, piping bag, baking tray, ice-cream scoop, wire cooling rack

Cookies
120 g plain flour
120 g cocoa powder, divided into 90 g and 30 g
1 teaspoon bicarbonate of soda
½ teaspoon salt
120 g unsalted butter
100 g sugar
110 g light brown sugar
1 egg
100 g icing sugar

Frosting
100 g icing sugar
1 tablespoon orange zest
¼ teaspoon salt
30 g unsalted butter, softened
¼ teaspoon vanilla extract
1 tablespoon orange juice

1. Whisk together the flour, 90 g cocoa powder, bicarbonate of soda and salt in a small bowl. Set aside.

2. Add the butter, sugar and light brown sugar to the bowl of a food mixer fitted with a paddle attachment. Beat on a medium speed until light and fluffy, about 5 to 7 minutes. Add the egg, and beat until incorporated, about 2 minutes.

3. Reduce the mixer speed to low and add the flour mixture. Continue beating on low until combined into a soft, sticky dough. Cover the bowl and chill the dough in the fridge for 3 hours.

4. While the dough chills, make the orange frosting. Add the icing sugar, orange zest, salt, butter and vanilla to a medium bowl. Beat with a hand mixer on low until smooth. Add the orange juice 1 teaspoon at a time, beating between each addition, until the frosting is smooth but still quite thick. Transfer the frosting to a piping bag, seal and set aside.

5. Towards the end of the dough chilling time, preheat the oven to 180°C. Line a baking tray with baking paper. Whisk the remaining 30 g cocoa powder with the icing sugar in a small bowl until combined.

6. Scoop 9 portions of cookie dough with an ice-cream scoop from the bowl. If you don't have an ice-cream scoop, measure out 2 tablespoons of mix to create a portion. Cover and chill the remaining dough. Roll each portion into a ball, then roll in the cocoa and icing sugar mixture until thickly coated. Place the balls on the prepared tray, leaving plenty of space between each cookie.

7. Bake the cookies for 10 to 13 minutes, until they have spread, puffed and set. If the cookies don't look craggy, give the tray a sharp tap on the countertop to deflate them and create their signature craggy appearance. Leave the cookies to cool for 5 minutes before transferring them to a wire rack to cool completely.

8. Repeat steps 6 and 7 with the remaining cookie dough. Trim off the tip of the piping bag so there is about a ½-cm opening. Pipe two large orange horns on to each cookie.

Floette
Focaccia

Focaccia is delicious on its own, but you can use toppings, such as mini peppers, cherry tomatoes, olives and fresh herbs, to turn your bake into a work of art. In this recipe, the toppings are arranged to look like a flower garden that Floette would love.

Difficulty: ● ● ● ○
Prep time: 35 minutes
Rest time: 5 hours
Bake time: 25 minutes
Dietary notes: Non-dairy, vegetarian

Equipment: Baking tray

600 ml lukewarm water
1 tablespoon honey
1 teaspoon active dry yeast
720 g plain flour
80 ml olive oil, plus more for the tray and drizzling
Fresh herbs, such as rosemary, thyme and chives
Red, yellow and orange cherry tomatoes
Mini peppers
Olives

1. Whisk together the water, honey and yeast in a large bowl. Leave to sit at room temperature until foamy, about 5 to 10 minutes. (If the mixture doesn't foam, the milk may be too warm. The ideal temperature should be between 40°C and 45°C. If it still doesn't foam, it's possible your yeast is dead, and you'll need to purchase new yeast.)

2. Add the flour and olive oil, then stir with a stiff plastic spatula or wooden spoon until no dry flour remains and a shaggy dough forms (the dough will be lumpy, with no dry flour remaining). Cover the bowl and leave the dough to sit at room temperature for 3 hours.

3. Pour enough olive oil in a baking tray to coat the bottom with a thin layer (about 3 to 4 tablespoons). Tilt the tray each way until the olive oil completely coats the bottom. Slide your hand under the top edge of the dough, and fold the dough in on itself. Turn the bowl and fold again, repeating the process 4 to 6 times.

4. Pour the dough into the prepared baking tray. Flip over the dough to coat both sides, and then spread the dough to the edges as far as you can. (Don't worry if the dough doesn't fill the tray all the way.) Drizzle more olive oil (1 to 2 tablespoons, or to taste) on top of the dough, then cover it with cling film. Leave the dough to rise for 2 more hours, until it is puffed and doubled in size.

5. Carefully stretch the dough to the edges of the tray, if needed, taking care not to deflate the dough too much.

6. Remove the tough, woody stems from the fresh herbs, leaving only tender stems and leaves. Cut some of the mini bell peppers crosswise to create small flowers, and cut some lengthwise into long spears to create petals for larger flowers.

7. Lay long chives along the long way of the tray to create stems. For longer stems, you can insert the fine points of some chives into the open end of other chives. Arrange the olives and cut peppers at the tips of the chives to create buds, small flowers and large flowers. Place cherry tomatoes along either side of the chives to create flowers. Arrange the remaining fresh herbs along the bottom of the flower garden, and along the chive stems, to create green bushes, grass and leaves for the flowers.

8. Bake the focaccia for 20 to 25 minutes, until golden brown. Drizzle with additional olive oil (2 to 3 tablespoons, or to taste). Leave to cool for 10 to 15 minutes before cutting and serving warm.

Alola Region

Pyukumuku Chocolate Roulade with Raspberry Whipped Cream

Mudbray Mud Pie

Comfey Tropical Pavlova

Mimikyu Chocolate Cupcakes with Praline Buttercream

Yungoos Toasted Coconut Chocolate Friands

Pyukumuku
Chocolate Roulade
with Raspberry Whipped Cream

This roulade is delicious, with a rich chocolate cake and a tangy raspberry filling that'll smack your tastebuds and make you smile. To top it all off, this cake is coated – but not with slime, like Pyukumuku! The sweet, pink, raspberry-flavoured whipped cream echoes the spikes on Pyukumuku's body and is a dazzling decoration, accompanied by a little whipped cream tail.

Difficulty: ● ● ● ○
Prep time: 30 minutes
Bake time: 25 minutes
Yield: Serves 8 to 10
Dietary notes: Gluten-free, vegetarian

Equipment: 22-by-33-cm baking tray, microwave, hand mixer, wire cooling rack, piping bag with large round tip

170 g dark chocolate
6 large eggs, separated
100 g sugar
½ teaspoon salt
30 g cocoa powder, sifted
480 ml double cream
25 g icing sugar
2 tablespoons raspberry powder

1. Preheat the oven to 180°C. Grease a 22-by-33-cm baking tray, then line it with baking paper so that there is a 5-cm overhang on both short ends.

2. Add the dark chocolate to a microwave-safe bowl. Heat in 30-second bursts, stirring each time, until the chocolate is melted and smooth. Set aside to cool slightly.

3. Using a hand mixer, beat 6 egg yolks with the sugar and salt in a medium bowl until the mixture is thickened and light in colour and the beaters leave ribbons behind them. With the beaters still going, slowly pour in the melted chocolate, beating until fully incorporated. Set aside.

4. Beat 6 egg whites in a large bowl with clean beaters (you can also do this in the bowl of a food mixer fitted with a whisk attachment) until firm peaks form. Using a plastic spatula, carefully fold the egg whites into the chocolate mixture, about a third at a time, until fully incorporated.

5. Sift the cocoa powder over the cake batter, and carefully fold it in with a plastic spatula until fully incorporated. Gently pour the batter into the prepared tray, gently spreading it evenly with the plastic spatula.

6. Bake for 25 minutes, until puffed and set. Lift the cake out of the tray and on to a wire rack. While the cake is still hot, carefully and gently roll it the long way into a tight roll, leaving the baking paper on the cake. Leave to cool completely.

7. While the cake cools, make the whipped cream. Beat together the double cream and icing sugar until medium peaks form. Reserve about 120 ml of the whipped cream in a small bowl, cover and chill. Add the raspberry powder to the remaining whipped cream and continue beating to stiff peaks. Cover and chill until the cake is ready to fill.

8. Transfer the raspberry whipped cream to a piping bag fitted with a large round tip. Carefully unroll the cake while gently peeling off the baking paper. Pipe a thin, even layer of the whipped cream on the unrolled cake, spreading with an offset spatula, if necessary. Reroll the cake and transfer it to a serving plate.

9. Pipe any remaining raspberry whipped cream in tall spikes all over the surface of the cake. Spoon the remaining plain whipped cream on one end of the top of the cake in a three-lobed puff, similar to Pyukumuku's tail. Slice the cake and serve immediately.

Mudbray
Mud Pie

Mudbray are happiest when they can make mud and play in the mire. Mud is certainly the inspiration for this pie, which hails from Mississippi in the USA. This pie is a must for chocolate fans: A chocolate biscuit crust, a rich brownie layer and a thick layer of luscious chocolate pudding, topped with mounds of whipped cream. These layers together resemble the mud that Mudbray loves so dearly.

Difficulty: ● ● ○ ○
Prep time: 45 minutes
Bake time: 40 minutes
Chill time: 4 hours
Yield: Serves 12
Dietary notes: Vegetarian

Equipment: 20-cm springform tin, small saucepan, wire cooling rack, medium saucier, hand mixer, grater

Crust

120 g unsalted butter, melted
300 g crushed chocolate biscuits
½ teaspoon salt

Brownie Layer

120 g unsalted butter
110 g dark chocolate
3 large eggs
110 g light brown sugar
50 g sugar
1 tablespoon vanilla extract
40 g plain flour
½ teaspoon salt
30 g cocoa powder, sifted
150 g chopped pecans, toasted

Pudding Layer

180 ml whole milk
180 ml double cream
2 tablespoons cornflour
140 g light brown sugar
¼ teaspoon salt
3 large egg yolks
110 g dark chocolate
30 g unsalted butter

Whipped Cream Layer

480 ml double cream
50 g icing sugar
Dark chocolate

To make the crust:

1. Preheat the oven to 180°C. Grease an 25-cm springform tin, then line the bottom with a circle of baking paper.

2. Stir together the butter, crushed biscuits and salt in a medium bowl until combined. Press the mixture into the bottom and completely up the sides of the tin. Use the flat bottom of a glass or cup to fully press the crust into the tin. Bake for 10 minutes. Set aside to cool while you make the brownie layer.

To make the brownie layer:

3. Add the butter and chocolate to a small saucepan, and melt over a low heat, stirring constantly, until smooth and incorporated. Set aside to cool.

4. Using a hand mixer, beat the eggs together with the brown sugar, sugar and vanilla in a large bowl until thickened and lighter in colour, about 5 minutes. While continuing to beat, slowly add the melted chocolate and butter mixture, beating until incorporated.

5. Reduce the mixer speed to low and add the flour, salt and cocoa, beating until just incorporated. Fold in the toasted pecans with a plastic spatula, then scrape the batter into the prepared crust. Bake for 25 to 30 minutes until just set and still slightly wobbly in the very centre. Let the brownie cool completely in the tin on a wire rack.

note: Sauciers have a curved bottom, which makes them preferable when a mixture will likely get trapped in the edges of a straight-sided saucepan. A saucepan is okay to use if you don't have a saucier, but you'll have to be extra vigilant and thorough with stirring so that the mixture doesn't get trapped in the edges and burn.

continued on the next page

To make the pudding layer:

6. Heat the milk and cream together in a medium saucier over a medium heat until just beginning to steam. Whisk together the cornflour, brown sugar, salt and egg yolks in a medium bowl until smooth.

7. While whisking continuously, very slowly pour the hot milk and cream into the egg yolk mixture. When all the milk and cream has been added, transfer the mixture back to the saucier. Cook over a medium heat, whisking gently but constantly, until the mixture begins to bubble. Once you see the first bubble, set a 1-minute timer and continue to whisk. Once the time is up, remove from heat.

8. Add the dark chocolate and butter to a medium bowl. Strain the milk mixture into the bowl. Leave to sit for a few minutes to allow the chocolate to melt, then stir until smooth. Cover with plastic wrap, pushing the cling film directly on to the surface of the pudding, and chill in the fridge for 4 hours.

To make the whipped cream:

9. Using a hand mixer, beat the double cream and icing sugar in a large bowl until medium peaks form. Set aside.

To assemble:

10. Stir the pudding until smooth, then pour it over the brownie layer, smoothing the top with a spatula. Top with the whipped cream, and smooth with a spatula. Grate a piece of dark chocolate all over the top. Keep covered and chilled and serve cold.

Comfey
Tropical Pavlova

Pavlovas are a versatile dessert that can be topped with whatever seasonal fruit is available. We decorate this pavlova with lots of fresh tropical fruit in a pattern that makes it look like a giant flower that any Comfey would be proud to use to adorn its vine.

Difficulty: ● ○ ○ ○
Prep time: 15 minutes
Bake time: 1 hour
Rest time: 1 hour
Yield: Serves 8 to 12
Dietary notes: Gluten-free, vegetarian

Equipment: Baking tray, food mixer, piping bag, wire cooling rack, hand mixer

4 large egg whites
¼ teaspoon cream of tartar
200 g sugar
½ teaspoon vanilla extract
240 ml double cream
1 tablespoon icing sugar
Strawberries, sliced
Pineapple, cut and sliced into thin wedges
Kiwis, peeled, quartered and thinly sliced
Mango, peeled, destoned and sliced into thin wedges

note: No matter what you use, it's important to use fresh fruit in a pavlova. Frozen fruit releases too many juices as it thaws that seep into the meringue layer and make it soggy.

1. Preheat the oven to 150°C. Line a baking tray with baking paper.

2. Beat together the egg whites and cream of tartar in a food mixer fitted with a whisk attachment until frothy. Increase the speed to medium-high, then slowly add the sugar. Continue whipping the egg whites until stiff peaks form. Add the vanilla and whip to combine.

3. Transfer the meringue to a piping bag. Trim off the tip to leave a 2½-cm opening at the end. To keep the baking paper from moving as you work, lift the corners of the baking paper in the tray and smear a tiny dollop on to the tray at all four corners. Press the baking paper down on to the meringue.

4. Pipe a 25-cm ring about 4 cm high. Pipe smaller concentric circles that are about 2½ cm high inside the 25-cm circle until it is completely filled in. If necessary, use an offset spatula to smooth the surface and fill in any gaps in the meringue.

5. Bake for 1 hour until set, but not browned. The meringue should look just off-white or cream-coloured. Turn off the oven. Prop open the oven door with a wooden spoon, and leave the meringue to sit in the warm oven for an additional hour. Remove from the oven and leave to cool completely in the tray set on a wire rack.

6. When the meringue base is completely cool, make the whipped cream. Using a hand mixer, beat together the cream and icing sugar until soft peaks form, about 5 minutes. Spread the whipped cream in the centre of the meringue, leaving the outermost ring bare.

7. Arrange the fruit in concentric circles, alternating colours for every circle, to make the pavlova look like a giant, multicoloured flower. Serve immediately.

note: An extremely versatile dessert, pavlova can be made year-round with fresh, seasonal fruits. Stone fruits, melons and berries in the summer; apples, figs and stone fruits for an autumnal treat; citrus fruits and cranberries in the winter; cherries, strawberries and citrus in the spring.

Mimikyu
Chocolate Cupcakes
with Praline Buttercream

Mimikyu wears a rag stitched together and decorated to look a bit like Pikachu, although that costume isn't fooling anyone. To contrast our bright, cheerful Pikachu cupcakes (page 19), we created a Mimikyu cupcake that mirrors its visual appearance, but with a very different flavour profile. The result is a cupcake that's full of dark and mysterious flavours.

Difficulty: ● ● ● ○
Prep time: 45 minutes
Bake time: 18 minutes
Yield: 12 cupcakes
Dietary notes: Vegetarian

Equipment: 12-hole muffin tray, small saucepan, food mixer, medium saucepan, hand mixer, four piping bags (one with a large round tip), palette knife, microwave, baking tray

Cupcakes
60 g dark chocolate
120 ml buttermilk
120 ml coffee
60 g cocoa powder
200 g sugar
60 ml neutral oil, such as vegetable or sunflower
2 eggs, room temperature
1 tablespoon vanilla extract
90 g plain flour
1 teaspoon salt
½ teaspoon baking powder
½ teaspoon bicarbonate of soda

Praline Buttercream
3 egg whites
150 g sugar
½ teaspoon salt
¼ teaspoon cream of tartar
210 g unsalted butter, softened
80 g praline paste

To Assemble
White chocolate
Dark chocolate
Red candy melts

To make the cupcakes:

1. Preheat the oven to 180°C. Line a standard muffin tray with 12 paper cupcake cases (preferably brown paper to complement Mimikyu's colours, but whatever you have is fine).

2. Add the dark chocolate, buttermilk and coffee to a small saucepan. Cook, stirring constantly, over a low heat until the chocolate is melted and the mixture is well combined. Stir in the cocoa powder until smooth, then remove from the heat. Leave to cool slightly.

3. Add the sugar and oil to the bowl of a food mixer fitted with a paddle attachment. Beat on a low speed to combine, then add the eggs and vanilla, beating until smooth. With the mixer running, slowly add the buttermilk mixture. Increase the mixer speed to medium and beat until smooth and slightly thickened, about 5 minutes.

4. Reduce the mixer speed to low, and add the flour, salt, baking powder and bicarbonate of soda. Beat until just combined, then turn off the mixer. Scrape down the sides and bottom of the bowl with a plastic spatula to make sure the batter is fully mixed.

5. Divide the batter between the cases and bake for 16 to 18 minutes, until a cake tester or toothpick inserted into the centre of the cupcakes comes out clean. Leave to cool completely.

continued on the next page

To make the praline buttercream:

6. While the cupcakes cool, make the buttercream. Fill a medium saucepan with about 1 cm of water. Set over a medium-low heat and allow it to come to a bare simmer. Add the egg whites, sugar, salt and cream of tartar to a metal mixing bowl. Place the bowl on top of the saucepan, ensuring that the bowl isn't touching the water. Heat the mixture, whisking constantly, until the sugar is completely dissolved. Remove from heat.

7. Beat the egg white mixture with a hand mixer until stiff peaks form and the mixture is room temperature, about 5 to 7 minutes. Add the softened butter, 2 tablespoons at a time, beating until fully incorporated before adding the next 2 tablespoons. The mixture may look soupy and curdled, but this is normal. Keep adding the butter and beating until the mixture is smooth and fluffy. Add the praline paste and beat to combine.

To assemble:

8. Transfer the buttercream to a piping bag fitted with a large round tip. Pipe a large round dollop of buttercream on top of each cupcake until all the buttercream is used up. If the piping tip leaves any points on the frosting, slightly wet a palette knife and smooth the frosting.

9. Add the white chocolate, dark chocolate and red candy melts to separate microwave-safe bowls. Working one at a time, heat each bowl in 30-second bursts, stirring each time, until all three are melted and smooth. Add a very small amount of dark chocolate to the white chocolate and stir to make a tan colour, adding more dark chocolate as needed to match the colouring of the buttercream. Transfer the two chocolates and candy melts to separate piping bags fitted with fine writing tips. (If you don't have enough tips, just snip off the very end of the piping bag tip to create a very small opening.)

10. Line a baking tray with baking paper. First, pipe the white chocolate mixture into 12 spear shapes to create the base for Mimikyu's straight ear. Then pipe 12 spears that are bent in the middle to create the base of Mimikyu's lopsided ear.

11. Pipe a small amount of dark chocolate on the tips of all 24 ears to complete them. Chill the ears in the freezer until set (5 to 10 minutes), then carefully peel them off the baking paper and insert them into the buttercream. Use the dark chocolate to pipe 2 messy spirals for Mimikyu's eyes directly on to each cupcake. Pipe a squiggly mouth on each cupcake with the dark chocolate.

12. Pipe 12 smaller messy scribbles beneath the eyes to create the red spots on Mimikyu's face.

Yungoos
Toasted Coconut Chocolate Friands

Friands are small, chewy almond cakes that originated in Australia. These rich, filling friands would sate even the hungriest Yungoos's appetite, and the creamy colour of the friand and chunks of chocolate match the brown colouring of its soft coat.

Difficulty: ● ○ ○ ○
Prep time: 10 minutes
Bake time: 25 minutes
Yield: 10 friands
Dietary notes: Vegetarian

Equipment: 12-hole muffin tray, wire cooling rack, microwave, two piping bags with small round tip and fine writing tip

120 g unsalted butter, melted and cooled
60 g plain flour
100 g almond flour
100 g toasted unsweetened coconut
5 large egg whites
100 g sugar
½ teaspoon salt
170 g dark chocolate, chopped
White chocolate
Dark chocolate

1. Preheat the oven to 180°C. Grease 10 holes in a standard muffin tray.

2. Stir together the butter, flour, almond flour and toasted coconut in a medium bowl.

3. Whisk together the egg whites, sugar and salt in a small bowl until frothy. Stir the egg white mixture into the flour mixture. Fold in the chopped chocolate.

4. Divide the friand batter among the prepared cups. Bake for 20 to 25 minutes, until golden and set. Leave the friands to cool in the tray for 10 minutes, then transfer to a wire cooling rack to cool completely.

5. Add the white chocolate and dark chocolate to separate microwave-safe bowls. Heat the bowls in the microwave, separately, in 30-second bursts, stirring each time, until the chocolates are melted and smooth. Transfer the white chocolate to a piping bag fitted with a small round tip and transfer the dark chocolate to a piping bag fitted with a fine writing tip.

6. Use the white chocolate to pipe a long oblong mouth shape across the bottom of each cooled friand in the white chocolate, making sure to fill in the shape completely. Pipe an outline in dark chocolate around the oblong shape, then pipe a dark chocolate zigzag across the length of the shape, to create Yungoos's teeth.

Galar Region

Dubwool Halva Brownies

Greedent Blueberry
Pecan Pie Bars

Yamper Mint Mocha Cake

Morpeko Double-Dipped
Viennese Cookies

Dubwool
Halva Brownies

Halva, a sweetened sesame treat, is normally quite dense and chewy, but when you crumble it up on to a hot brownie and bake for a minute or two, it melts and puffs up into a fluffy texture, just like Dubwool's coat. The nutty halva pairs beautifully with the dark chocolate brownie, creating a simple dessert that tastes complex, like it took much longer to make than it did.

Difficulty: ● ○ ○ ○
Prep time: 10 minutes
Bake time: 25 minutes
Yield: 16 brownies
Dietary notes: Vegetarian

Equipment: 20-by-20-cm baking tin, small saucepan, hand mixer

120 g unsalted butter
110 g dark chocolate
110 g light brown sugar
50 g sugar
1 tablespoon vanilla
3 large eggs
40 g plain flour
30 g cocoa powder
½ teaspoon salt
Plain halva
Chocolate halva

1. Preheat the oven to 180°C. Grease a 20-by-20-cm baking tin, then line it with baking paper, so that there's a 5-cm overhang on two sides.

2. Gently heat the butter and dark chocolate in a small saucepan over a low heat until melted and smooth. Remove from heat and set aside to cool down slightly.

3. Using a hand mixer, beat the chocolate mixture with the brown sugar, sugar and vanilla in a medium bowl until smooth, about 5 minutes. Add the eggs all at once and beat until the mixture is combined and smooth.

4. Reduce the mixer speed to low, and add the flour, cocoa and salt, beating just to combine. Scrape the batter into the prepared tin and bake for about 23 minutes until just set – it will have a glossy top and be slightly wobbly in the centre.

5. Crumble the plain halva all over the hot brownies. Crumble a smaller amount of the chocolate halva here and there over the plain halva. Return the tin to the oven until the halva is melted and slightly puffed, about 2 minutes more. Cool in the tin to room temperature.

6. Lift the cooled brownies out of the tin and transfer them to a chopping board. Cut into 16 brownies and serve.

Greedent
Blueberry Pecan Pie Bars

Greedent love to store berries in their tail. They particularly love Oran Berries, which resemble plump, juicy blueberries. We similarly hid a ton of blueberries in a tray of these pecan pie bars, and the result was a chewy, gooey, fruity filling on top of a crunchy crust. The toasty brown pecans are the cherry (or blueberry) on top, creating a nice crunch and a rich colour reminiscent of Greedent's fluffy fur.

Difficulty: ● ● ○ ○
Prep time: 20 minutes
Bake time: 1 hour
Yield: 18 bars
Dietary notes: Vegetarian

Equipment: 22-by-33-inch baking tin, wire cooling rack

Crust
240 g plain flour
100 g pecan flour
55 g light brown sugar
¾ teaspoon salt
150 g unsalted butter, melted

Filling
4 eggs
225 g honey
225 g maple syrup
1 tablespoon vanilla extract
2 tablespoons cornflour
1 teaspoon salt
60 g unsalted butter, melted
340 g blueberries, fresh or frozen
(no need to thaw)
225 g chopped pecans

1. Preheat the oven to 180°C. Grease a 22-by-33-cm baking tin. Line with baking paper so there's a 5-cm overhang on the long sides of the tin.

2. Make the crust. Stir together the flour, pecan flour, brown sugar and salt until combined. Stir in the butter until thoroughly mixed in. Press the crust into the bottom of the baking tin, using the flat bottom of a glass or cup to compress the crust. Bake for 12 minutes, until lightly golden and set.

3. Whisk together the eggs, honey, maple syrup, vanilla, cornflour, salt and butter until smooth. Fold in the blueberries and pecans until evenly dispersed. Pour it over the crust and bake until set, about 45 minutes.

4. Set the tin on a wire rack and leave the pie to cool completely. Loosen the edges with a thin knife, then lift the pie out of the baking tin. Transfer to a chopping board and cut into 18 bars.

Yamper
Mint Mocha Cake

Yamper is such a glutton for treats that it'll only help its Trainer in exchange for snacks. If you're trying to get your friends to help you with a big task, offer them this treat. This bright green, mint-flavoured cake, its fluffy mocha buttercream and the cute fondant details create the colours of Yamper's soft coat. Finish it off with a lightning bolt for this crackling Puppy Pokémon and you've got a masterpiece no one will turn down!

Difficulty: ● ● ○ ○
Prep Time: 45 minutes
Bake Time: 30 minutes
Yield: Serves 12 to 16
Dietary notes: Vegetarian

Equipment: Two 20-cm round cake tins, food mixer, wire cooling rack, medium saucepan, hand mixer, offset spatula, two heart-shaped biscuit cutters (one about 6½ cm long, one about 4½ cm inches long)

Cake

300 g sugar
1 tablespoon baking powder
1 teaspoon salt
180 g unsalted butter, softened
2 large eggs, room temperature
1 tablespoon vanilla extract
1½ teaspoons mint extract
3 to 5 drops green food colouring (optional)
270 g plain flour
320 ml whole milk, room temperature

Mocha Buttercream

3 egg whites
150 g sugar
½ teaspoon salt
¼ teaspoon cream of tartar
210 g unsalted butter, softened
90 g dark chocolate, melted and cooled
1 teaspoon espresso powder mixed
with 1 teaspoon hot water

Decorations

Pale green fondant
Pale yellow fondant
Icing sugar, for dusting

To make the cake:

1. Preheat the oven to 180°C. Grease two 20-cm round cake tin, then line the bottoms with circles of baking paper. Grease the baking paper.

2. Add the sugar, baking powder, salt and butter to the bowl of a food mixer fitted with a paddle attachment. Mix on a low speed until moistened, then increase the speed to medium-high and beat until light and fluffy, 5 to 7 minutes, scraping down the sides of the bowl with a plastic spatula about halfway through.

3. Add the eggs, one at a time, beating to incorporate fully before adding the next egg. Add the vanilla and mint extracts and the food colouring (if using), beating to combine.

4. Reduce the mixer speed to low, then add a third of the flour and beat to combine. Pour in half the milk and beat until smooth. Repeat, adding a third of the flour and the remaining milk; end with the last of the flour, beating just until incorporated and scraping down the bowl and paddle with a plastic spatula as necessary.

5. Divide the batter between the two cake tins, spreading the batter evenly. Bake for 30 minutes, until a cake tester inserted into the centre of the cakes comes out mostly clean, with just a few moist crumbs clinging to it. Let the cakes cool in the tins for about 10 minutes before turning them out on to a wire rack to cool completely.

To make the buttercream:

6. While the cakes cool, make the buttercream. Fill a medium saucepan with about 1 cm of water. Set over a medium-low heat and allow the water to come to a bare simmer. Add the egg whites, sugar, salt and cream of tartar to a metal mixing bowl. Place the bowl on top of the saucepan, ensuring that the bowl isn't touching the water. Heat the mixture, whisking constantly, until the sugar is completely dissolved. Remove from heat.

continued on the next page

7. Beat the egg white mixture with a hand mixer on high until stiff peaks form and the mixture is room temperature, about 5 to 7 minutes. Add the softened butter, 2 tablespoons at a time, beating until fully incorporated, before adding the next 2 tablespoons. The mixture may look soupy and curdled, but this is normal. Keep adding the butter and beating until the mixture is smooth and fluffy.

8. Add the melted chocolate and espresso to the buttercream and beat to combine to make the mocha buttercream.

To decorate:

9. Place one of the cooled cakes on a serving plate. Spread about 1 cup of mocha buttercream on top, then place the second cake on top. Spread the remaining mocha buttercream on the top and sides of the cake. Smooth the top and sides with an offset spatula.

10. Knead the pale green and pale yellow fondants separately on a clean, dry surface until smooth and pliable. Lightly dust the surface with icing sugar and roll out the fondant (about 2 mm thick). Using the larger heart-shaped cookie cutter (about 6 cm in length), cut out 16 hearts out of the pale green fondant. Repeat with the pale yellow fondant, using a smaller heart-shaped cookie cutter (about 4½ cm inches in length).

11. From the yellow fondant, cut out the lightning bolt in the shape of Yamper's tail (about 10 to 12 cm tall and 5 to 7½ cm wide). Cut a long strip of yellow fondant to make the base decoration. Use a sharp knife or a pizza cutter to make the wavy top. Carefully press around the cake, trimming to fit and smoothing out the seam. Place the hearts evenly around the cake, pressing the yellow hearts in the centre of the green hearts. Finish with the lightning-bolt tail in the middle.

Morpeko
Double-Dipped Viennese Cookies

Morpeko can get irritable when it's hungry, which is almost always! To stay fed, Morpeko carries electrically roasted seeds, which it treasures. Once you taste the melt-in-your-mouth cookies, you'll consider them your own treasure. It's dipped in decadent dark chocolate to reflect the Electric- and Dark-type Pokémon.

Difficulty: ● ○ ○ ○
Prep time: 15 minutes
Bake time: 15 minutes
Chill time: 30 minutes
Yield: 12 cookies
Dietary notes: Vegetarian

Equipment: Baking tray, hand mixer, piping bag with large star tip, wire cooling rack, microwave

120 g unsalted butter, softened
25 g icing sugar
¼ teaspoon salt
1 teaspoon vanilla paste (or extract)
120 g plain flour
2 tablespoons cornflour
110 g dark chocolate
110 g milk chocolate

1. Preheat the oven to 190°C. Line a baking tray with baking paper.

2. Using a hand mixer, beat the butter, icing sugar, salt and vanilla paste on a low speed in a medium bowl until moistened. Increase the speed to medium-high and beat until light and fluffy, about 5 to 7 minutes.

3. Sift together the flour and cornflour over the butter mixture. Mix on a low speed until moistened, then increase the speed to medium and mix until smooth and just incorporated. Transfer the dough to a piping bag fitted with a large star tip.

4. Pipe 12 large, closed figure of eights on to the baking paper, leaving about an 1½ cm between each one. Chill the entire baking tray in the fridge for 30 minutes – this will help the cookies keep their shape while baking. If you're in a rush, you can freeze the dough for about 10 to 15 minutes.

5. Bake the cookies for 12 to 15 minutes until set and lightly golden. Let the cookies cool on the tray for 5 minutes, then transfer them to a wire rack to cool completely. Reserve the baking paper-lined tray.

6. Add the dark and milk chocolates to separate microwave-safe bowls. Microwave each bowl separately in 30-second bursts, stirring each time, until the chocolate is melted and smooth.

7. Grip a cookie in the centre and dip one long side into the milk chocolate, allowing the excess to drip off before dipping the other side into the dark chocolate, leaving the middle of the cookie bare. Allow the excess dark chocolate to drip off the cookie, then set it on the reserved tray to set. Repeat with the remaining cookies. Let the chocolate set, then serve.

PALDEA REGION

Sprigatito Pistachio Rose Rolls

Quaxly Blueberry Buckle

Fuecoco Spiced Ginger Loaf

Koraidon Mixed Berry Soufflé

Miraidon Lemon Cheesecake
& Ube Cake

Sprigatito
Pistachio Rose Rolls

Sprigatito gives off a scent that mesmerises those around it. These rose-scented, pistachio-filled rolls have a similar effect. The edible rose petals scattered over the top – soft pink, like Sprigatito's eyes – would make any Grass-type Pokémon happy. This recipe uses the tangzhong technique, which involves gelatinising some of the flour before incorporating it into the dough. This improves the texture of the bread.

Difficulty: ● ● ● ○
Prep time: 30 minutes
Rest time: 2 hours
Bake time: 25 minutes
Yield: 12 rolls
Dietary notes: Vegetarian

Equipment: Small saucepan, food mixer, 30-cm cast-iron pan, instant-read thermometer

Tangzhong
240 g plain flour
60 ml whole milk

Dough
480 g plain flour
1½ teaspoons salt
2 teaspoons instant yeast
55 g brown sugar
240 ml whole milk
2 large eggs
60 g unsalted butter, softened

Filling
170 g pistachio paste
90 g unsalted butter, melted
25 g icing sugar
2 tablespoons honey
1 tablespoon brown sugar

Icing
150 g icing sugar
1 tablespoon orange juice
30 ml double cream
½ teaspoon rose water
2 drops green food colouring (optional)

To Finish
Dried edible rose petals
Chopped pistachios

To make the tangzhong:

1. Whisk together the flour and milk in a small saucepan set over a low heat. Cook until the mixture takes on a pudding-like consistency, about 3 minutes. Leave to cool.

To make the dough:

2. Add the flour, salt, yeast and brown sugar to the bowl of a food mixer fitted with a dough hook attachment. Mix on a low speed to combine, then add the milk, both eggs and the cooled tangzhong, mixing until a shaggy dough forms. Increase the mixer speed to medium-high and knead until smooth.

3. Add half the butter to the bowl and allow it to fully incorporate. Add the remaining butter. Continue kneading for 15 additional minutes, until the dough is smooth and elastic. Cover the dough and let it rise for about 1 hour, until puffed and doubled in size.

To make the filling:

4. Meanwhile, make the filling by stirring together the pistachio paste and butter in a small bowl until smooth. Mix in the icing sugar, honey and brown sugar until smooth.

To assemble the rolls:

5. Preheat the oven to 180°C. Grease a 30-cm cast-iron pan.

6. When the dough has risen, gently punch it down to deflate, then turn it out on to a floured work surface. Roll the dough to a 50-by-30-cm rectangle. Spread the filling evenly over the surface of the dough, leaving a 1-cm border on both short edges and one long edge.

note: If you're unsure whether the dough is ready, tear off a small chunk. Stretch the dough – if you can stretch it enough to see through it without the dough tearing, it's ready to go. If the dough tears, continue mixing for 5 more minutes, then test it again. (This is called the windowpane test.)

continued on the next page

7. Roll the dough into a tight coil, rolling towards the bare-bordered long edge. Pinch the seam to seal. Trim 2½ cm off both ends to make an 45-cm-long log. Cut twelve 4-cm-thick rounds and place them in the prepared tray, spacing them evenly. Cover the rounds and let them rise for about 1 hour, until they're puffed and crowding each other.

8. Bake the rolls for 25 minutes, until they're golden brown and an instant-read thermometer registers 90°C when inserted into the centre of the rolls. Leave to cool slightly.

To make the icing and finish:

9. While the rolls cool, make the icing by combining the icing sugar, orange juice, cream, rose water and food colouring (if using) in a small bowl until smooth. Pour over the rolls while warm, spreading evenly. Scatter edible rose petals and chopped pistachios over the top and serve warm or at room temperature.

Quaxly
Blueberry Buckle

A buckle is a rich, dense cake (sort of like a coffee cake) packed with fruit, and this buckle is particularly fashionable! Quaxly uses cream as a styling product to keep the coif on its head slicked back, so we top each slice of this delicious blueberry buckle with coifs of blueberry-flavoured whipped cream to honour this stylish Pokémon.

Difficulty: ● ○ ○ ○
Prep time: 15 minutes
Bake time: 45 minutes
Yield: Serves 9
Dietary notes: Vegetarian

Equipment: 20-by-20-cm baking tin, hand mixer, wire cooling rack

Streusel Topping
110 g light brown sugar
60 g plain flour
1 teaspoon cinnamon
¼ teaspoon nutmeg
¼ teaspoon salt
60 g unsalted butter, melted

Buckle
240 g plain flour
2 teaspoons baking powder
½ teaspoon salt
90 g unsalted butter, softened
100 g sugar
2 eggs
120 ml sour cream
280 g blueberries (fresh or frozen, no need to thaw)

Whipped Cream
240 ml double cream
1 tablespoon sugar
2 teaspoons blueberry powder, or 1 tablespoon blueberry juice

1. Preheat the oven to 190°C. Grease an 20-by-20-cm baking tin.

2. Make the streusel topping by stirring together all the ingredients in a small bowl until it resembles wet sand. Set aside.

3. Make the buckle. Whisk together the flour, baking powder and salt in a small bowl.

4. Using a hand mixer on a medium speed, beat together the butter and sugar in a medium bowl for about 5 to 7 minutes, until light and fluffy. Beat in the eggs, mixing until smooth.

5. Reduce the mixer speed to low, and add half the flour mixture, mixing until just combined. Add the sour cream and mix until smooth, then add the remaining flour mixture. Mix until just incorporated. Gently fold the blueberries into the batter using a plastic spatula.

6. Pour the batter into the prepared tin and spread it evenly. Sprinkle the streusel topping all over the top. Bake for 45 minutes until golden brown and a cake tester inserted into the centre of the buckle comes out clean (blueberry juice doesn't count!). Place the tin on a wire rack and leave the buckle to cool in the tin to room temperature.

7. Whip the double cream, sugar and blueberry powder in a medium bowl until medium peaks form. Cut the blueberry buckle, and serve each slice with a tall dollop of blueberry whipped cream, sweeping some of the dollop in front to the right to emulate Quaxly's signature hairstyle. Store any leftover whipped cream and buckle separately: Keep the whipped cream covered and in the fridge, and keep the buckle covered at room temperature.

Fuecoco
Spiced Ginger Loaf

Fuecoco stores fire energy in the scales on its stomach, then releases it from the dent on top of its head. This spicy ginger loaf is packed with so many delicious warming spices and is topped with candied ginger to emulate Fuecoco's leaking fire energy.

Difficulty: ● ○ ○ ○
Prep time: 15 minutes
Bake time: 40 minutes
Yield: Serves 8 to 12
Dietary notes: Vegetarian

Equipment: 22-by-12-cm loaf tin, food mixer, instant-read thermometer, wire cooling rack

Loaf
120 g unsalted butter, softened
60 g honey or molasses
165 g light brown sugar
2 large eggs, room temperature
120 ml buttermilk, room temperature
1 tablespoon vanilla extract
240 g plain flour
2 teaspoons baking powder
1 teaspoon ground ginger
2 teaspoons cinnamon
¼ teaspoon ground cloves
¼ teaspoon allspice
¼ teaspoon cayenne
¼ teaspoon nutmeg

Icing
100 g icing sugar
½ teaspoon cinnamon
2 tablespoons milk
4 to 6 drops red food colouring (optional)
Yellow food colouring (optional)

Decoration
Candied ginger, cut into 2 long strips

1. Preheat the oven to 180°C. Grease a 22-by-12-cm loaf tin.

2. In the bowl of a food mixer fitted with a paddle attachment, beat together the butter, honey and brown sugar on a medium speed until light and fluffy. Mix in the eggs until fully incorporated, followed by the buttermilk and vanilla.

3. Reduce the mixer speed to low, and add the flour, baking powder, ginger, cinnamon, cloves, allspice, cayenne and nutmeg. Mix until combined.

4. Scrape the batter into the prepared tin, and bake for 40 minutes, until an instant-read thermometer inserted into the centre of the loaf registers 90°C. Leave the cake to cool in the tin for 5 minutes before turning out on to a wire rack to cool completely.

5. For the icing, mix the icing sugar, cinnamon and milk together until smooth and thick. If using food colouring, divide the icing into thirds, separating each third into a clean bowl. Add 3 to 5 drops of red food colouring to one bowl to create red icing, 1 drop red food colouring and 3 to 5 drops yellow food colouring to the second bowl to create orange icing, and 4 to 6 drops yellow food colouring to the third bowl to create yellow icing. Stir each icing until uniform in colour.

6. Pour over the top of the loaf in a flame shape, starting with the yellow icing, then accenting with orange and red icing to create flame patterns however you'd like, allowing the excess to drip down the sides of the loaf. If needed, shape the icing into the flame shape or feather through the colours with the sharp tip of a knife.

7. Poke one hole in the centre of the loaf with a chopstick. Insert one long strip and one shorter strip of candied ginger into the hole to create the leaking fire energy on Fuecoco's head.

Koraidon
Mixed Berry Soufflé

Soufflés are notorious for being one of the most difficult desserts to make – a challenge befitting a Legendary Pokémon, like Koraidon. You must leave the oven door closed for the entire baking process, or the delicate soufflé will sink. This soufflé is extra difficult to make because it requires two separate purées to be gently combined and swirled before baking. The purées are also drizzled on the top to mirror Koraidon's colouring.

Difficulty: ● ● ● ●
Prep time: 30 minutes
Bake time: 30 minutes
Yield: Serves 4 to 6
Dietary notes: Gluten-free, non-dairy, vegetarian

Equipment: 960-g soufflé dish, small saucepan, blender, hand mixer, cooking string, paper clip

110 g frozen blueberries
110 g frozen blackberries
170 g frozen strawberries
110 g frozen raspberries
4 large eggs, separated
100 g sugar, plus 2 tablespoons sugar for the soufflé dish
2 teaspoons cornflour
1 tablespoon lemon juice
¼ teaspoon salt

note: A soufflé dish is a straight-sided, heatproof baking dish used specifically for making soufflés. It's typically made from porcelain, and the straight, tall sides help soufflés achieve their signature rise.

1. Preheat the oven to 200°C. Butter the inside of a 960-g soufflé dish. Sprinkle 2 tablespoons sugar inside. Rotate the dish to evenly coat, then tip out the excess.

2. Add the blueberries and blackberries to a small saucepan. Cook on a medium-low heat, stirring occasionally, until the berries break down and release their juices, about 5 to 7 minutes. Leave to cool.

3. Repeat step 2 with the strawberries and raspberries.

4. Add the blueberry mixture to a blender and blend on a high speed until smooth. Strain, then measure a quarter of a cup of purée into a small bowl; reserve the rest to serve. Rinse out the blender, and repeat the process with the strawberry mixture, keeping the berry purées separate. Set aside.

5. Using a hand mixer on a high speed, beat the egg yolks with the sugar in a medium bowl for about 8 minutes, until the yolks are thick and light and the beaters leave ribbons as you move them through the bowl.

6. Whisk together the cornflour and lemon juice in a small bowl until smooth, then beat it into the egg yolk mixture, along with the salt. Divide this mixture into two medium bowls. Stir the blueberry/blackberry purée into one of the bowls, then stir the strawberry/raspberry purée into the other.

7. Whip the egg whites in a large bowl with a clean hand mixer until stiff peaks form. (It is extremely important that the beaters be completely clean, or the egg whites won't whip to the correct consistency.)

8. Quickly and gently fold half the whipped egg whites into the blueberry mixture using a plastic spatula until just incorporated. Fold the remaining whipped egg whites into the strawberry mixture.

continued on the next page

9. Simultaneously pour both batters into the prepared soufflé dish. Using a butter knife, carefully swirl the two mixtures together (this will also knock out any large pockets of air in the batter, but be careful not to overdo it – six passes through the batter should be plenty).

10. Quickly spray a thin layer of cooking spray on to a sheet of baking paper, then use the baking paper to create a collar by wrapping it around the soufflé dish and securing it with cooking string. The collar should extend 10 cm past the top of the soufflé dish. Secure the overlapping seam at the top of the baking paper with a paper clip.

11. Bake for 30 minutes, until the soufflé is puffed, risen and lightly browned on top. Carefully remove the baking paper collar and serve immediately, before the soufflé collapses. Drizzle each serving with the remaining berry purées.

Miraidon
Lemon Cheesecake & Ube Cake

It's time to put your Pokémon baking skills to the test. As with battling a Legendary Pokémon, this recipe requires you to use many precise skills and techniques. You'll feel powerful when you make this epic dessert, which is worthy of the Iron Serpent!

Difficulty: ● ● ● ●
Prep time: 1½ hours
Bake time: 1 hour and 25 minutes
Chill time: 4 hours
Yield: Serves 12 to 16
Dietary notes: Vegetarian

Equipment: 20-cm springform tin, food mixer, wire cooling rack, two 20-cm round cake tins, hand mixer, piping bag with small round tip

Cheesecake
Two 225-g tubs cream cheese, softened
120 ml sour cream, room temperature
100 g sugar
2 teaspoons vanilla extract
2 teaspoons lemon zest
2 large eggs, room temperature
2 tablespoons lemon juice
1 tablespoon plain flour
1 tablespoon cornflour

Ube Cakes
300 g sugar
240 ml neutral oil, such as vegetable or sunflower
120 g unsalted butter, softened
2 large eggs
2 teaspoons vanilla extract
1 tablespoon ube extract
300 g self-raising flour
1½ teaspoons bicarbonate of soda
1 teaspoon salt
240 ml buttermilk

note: Ube is a bright purple yam, similar to a sweet potato. It pairs well with not only lemon, but also other sweets, such as vanilla, coconut, mango, guava, passion fruit and even cheese! A good replacement is purple food colouring.

To make the lemon cheesecake:

1. Preheat oven to 165°C. Grease an 20-cm springform tin, and line the bottom of the tin with a circle of baking paper.

2. Beat the cream cheese, sour cream, sugar, vanilla and lemon zest in the bowl of a food mixer on a medium-low speed until smooth. Beat in the eggs, one at a time, beating until fully incorporated before adding the next egg.

3. Whisk together the lemon juice with the flour and cornflour in a small bowl until smooth. Beat into the cream cheese mixture until incorporated.

4. Pour the cheesecake batter into the prepared springform tin, smoothing the top with a plastic spatula. Bake for 45 to 55 minutes, until lightly golden and set, with just a slight wobble in the centre. Turn off the oven, and prop open the door with a wooden spoon, allowing the cheesecake to slowly cool in the warm oven for 30 minutes before transferring the tin to a wire rack to cool completely. Cover and chill the tin for 4 hours.

To make the ube cakes:

5. Preheat the oven to 180°C. Grease two 20-cm cake tins, then line the bottoms with circles of baking paper.

6. In the bowl of a food mixer fitted with a paddle attachment, cream the sugar, oil and butter together until smooth, about 5 minutes. Add the eggs one at a time, beating to incorporate before adding the next egg. Mix in the vanilla and ube extracts, beating until evenly coloured.

7. Sift together the cake flour, bicarbonate of soda and salt into a small bowl. Add a third of the flour mixture to the batter, mixing on low until just incorporated. Add half the buttermilk, mixing until smooth, then repeat the process with the remaining flour mixture and buttermilk, ending with the flour mixture.

8. Divide the batter between the prepared cake tins, spreading evenly. Bake for 30 minutes, until a cake tester inserted into the centre of the cake comes out clean, with just a few moist crumbs clinging to it.

9. Leave the cakes to cool in the tins for 10 minutes before turning them out on to a wire rack to cool completely.

continued on the next page

Frosting

Two 225-g tubs of cream cheese, softened

240 g unsalted butter, softened

2 teaspoons lemon zest

2 teaspoons vanilla extract

300 g icing sugar

30 ml double cream,
plus more if needed

6 drops yellow food colouring

1 to 3 drops ube extract (see note
on page 135)

Silver ball decorations

note: If you'd like exceptionally clean lines when creating the tyre track pattern, you can use pale purple and white fondant instead. Lay them over the yellow frosting, then press in the silver sugar balls as described.

To make the frosting:

10. Using a hand mixer on a medium speed, beat together the cream cheese and butter in a large bowl until completely smooth. Mix in the lemon zest and vanilla until combined.

11. Reduce the mixer speed to low and add the icing sugar 100 g at a time, mixing until moistened. Add the double cream, increase the speed to medium-high, and mix until smooth, about 8 to 10 minutes. If the frosting is too thick, add more double cream as needed until it reaches a soft, spreadable consistency but still holds its shape.

12. Remove half a cup of frosting and transfer to a separate bowl, then remove a second half cup of frosting and transfer that to another separate bowl. Add 4 to 6 drops yellow food colouring to the largest amount of frosting, and beat until uniform in colour. If needed, add more yellow food colouring to closer match Miraidon's colouring. Add 1 drop of ube extract to one of the bowls with half a cup of reserved frosting. Stir to combine to make pale purple frosting. If needed, add an additional drop or two of ube extract to match Miraidon's light purple colouring. Leave the remaining half cup of reserved frosting uncoloured.

To assemble:

13. If the ube cakes have domed, trim off the tops with a serrated knife so they are flat and level. (It is very important that the cakes are level; otherwise, the cake might fall over!)

14. Place one of the ube cakes on a serving plate. Spread three quarters of a cup of yellow frosting over the top of the cake. Use a paring knife to loosen the cheesecake from the sides of the springform tin. Release and remove the body of the springform tin, then place a plate on top of the cheesecake. Invert the cheesecake, peel off the baking paper, then place the cheesecake on top of the frosted cake. Spread three quarters of a cup of yellow frosting over the top of the cheesecake. Add the final layer of cake and spread the remaining yellow frosting over the top and sides of the cake. Spread the light purple frosting in a thick line over the cake to create Miraidon's belly, extending down the cake sides.

15. Fill a piping bag with the reserved uncoloured frosting fitted with a small round tip. Pipe the white tread marks on Miraidon's belly on the cake across the light purple frosting, and extending slightly over on to the yellow frosting. Carefully place 20 or so silver ball decorations all around the light purple part of the cake to mimic the sparkles on Miraidon's belly.

Measurement Conversions

VOLUME

Metric	US
1 ml	⅕ teaspoon
5 ml	1 teaspoon
15 ml	1 tablespoon
30 ml	1 fluid ounce
50 ml	⅕ cup
60 ml	¼ cup
80 ml	⅓ cup
100 ml	3.4 fluid ounces
120 ml	½ cup
160 ml	⅔ cup
180 ml	¾ cup
240 ml	1 cup
480 ml	1 pint (2 cups)
.95 liter	1 quart (4 cups)

TEMPERATURES

Celsius	Fahrenheit
93.3°	200°
100°	212°
120°	250°
135°	275°
150°	300°
163°	325°
177°	350°
205°	400°
218°	425°
232°	450°
246°	475°

WEIGHT

Metric	US
14 grams	0.5 ounce
28 grams	1 ounce
113 grams	¼ pound
151 grams	⅓ pound
227 grams	½ pound
454 grams	1 pound

Dietary Considerations

Recipe	Page	Gluten-Free	Non-dairy	Vegetarian
Bidoof – Peanut Butter Pretzel Tart	59			X
Blissey – Strawberry Twists	37			X
Buizel – Apricot Thumbprint Cookies	71			X
Charmander – Brown Butter Marmalade Financiers	15			X
Chespin – Raspberry Pistachio Napoleon	91			X
Chikorita – Cheesy Pesto Brioche Rolls	31			X*
Combee – Honey Cake	63			X
Comfey – Tropical Pavlova	107	X		X
Dedenne – Mango-Gingerbread Pudding	93			X
Delibird – Red Velvet Cake with Peppermint Cream Cheese Frosting	34			X
Doduo – Chocolate Macaroons	17	X	X	X
Drifloon – Blackberry Galette	67			X
Dubwool – Halva Brownies	114			X
Floette – Focaccia	97		X	X
Flygon – Pan Pizza	55			X
Fuecoco – Spiced Ginger Loaf	129			X
Gastrodon – Cheesecake Swirl Bars with Chocolate Streusel	68			X
Greedent – Blueberry Pecan Pie Bars	115			X
Igglybuff – Chocolate Raspberry Cupcakes	33			X
Koraidon – Mixed Berry Soufflé	131	X	X	X
Kricketot – Chocolate Strawberry Sandwich Cookies	65			X
Magby – Spicy Cherry Tomato Galette	39			X*
Mimikyu – Chocolate Cupcakes with Praline Buttercream	109			X
Miraidon – Lemon Cheesecake & Ube Cake	135			X
Morpeko – Double-Dipped Viennese Cookies	121			X
Mudbray – Mud Pie	103			X
Oshawott – Blueberry Meringue Tartlets	77			X
Phanpy – Orange Cream Tartlets	27			X
Pikachu – Tropical Cupcakes	19			X
Poké Ball – Conchas	13			X
Ponyta – Cinnamon Panna Cotta	22	X		X
Pyroar – Spicy Pumpkin Empanadas	94			X
Pyukumuku – Chocolate Roulade with Raspberry Whipped Cream	101	X		X
Quaxly – Blueberry Buckle	127			X
Sandile – Butterscotch & Brownie Parfait	81			X
Scraggy – Orange Cardamom Sweet Rolls	83			X
Seedot – Black Sesame Swirl Cake	43			X
Shellder – Madeleines	23			X
Snivy – Lemon Biscotti with Chocolate, Pistachios & Candied Lemon Peel	74			X
Spoink – Black Sesame Cream Puffs	53			X
Sprigatito – Pistachio Rose Rolls	125			X
Taillow – Chocolate Cherry Olive Oil Cake	47			X
Tepig – Spiced Chocolate Bundt Cake	75			X
Togepi – Confetti Mug Cake	29			X
Tyrunt – Chocolate Crinkle Cookies	95			X
Whimsicott – Angel Food Cake	85			X
Whismur – Lemon-Lavender Bars	49			X
Yamper – Mint Mocha Cake	117			X
Yungoos – Toasted Coconut Chocolate Friands	111			X
Zigzagoon – Mocha Éclairs	45			X

Difficulty Index

About the Author

Jarrett Melendez grew up on the mean, deer-infested streets of Bucksport, Maine. A former chef and line cook, Jarrett has worked in restaurants, diners and bakeries throughout New England and Mexico, and got instruction on Japanese home cooking from some very patient host mothers when he lived in Tokyo and Hiroshima. He's been a professional writer since 2009, but started working as a recipe developer and food writer in 2020. His work has appeared on *Bon Appétit*, *Saveur*, *Epicurious* and *Food52*, and he is the author of *The Comic Kitchen*, an upcoming fully illustrated, comic-style cookbook. When not cooking and writing about food, Jarrett is also an award-winning comic book writer. His best known work is *Chef's Kiss* from Oni Press, which won the Alex Award from the American Library Association, along with a GLAAD award nomination for Outstanding Graphic Novel. Jarrett has contributed to the Ringo-nominated *All We Ever Wanted*, *Full Bleed*, *Young Men in Love* and *Murder Hobo: Chaotic Neutral*. He is currently working on *Tales of the Fungo: The Legend of Cep*, a middle-grade fantasy adventure, to be published by Andrews McMeel. He lives in Massachusetts with his collection of Monokuro Boo plush pigs.